THE —
WORLD'S BEST RESTAURANTS

D1324013

In association with

THE
S.PELLEGRINO
WORLD'S
50
BEST
RESTAURANTS

First published in 2008 by Think Books, an imprint of Pan Macmillan Ltd
Pan Macmillan, 20 New Wharf Road, London N1 9RR, Basingstoke and Oxford
Associated companies throughout the world
www.panmacmillan.com
www.think-books.com

ISBN: 978-1-84525-057-7

Text © Pan Macmillan Ltd.
Design © Think Publishing and William Reed Publishing

Editor: Emma Jones
Design: Dominic Scott
Contributors: Tania Adams, Andrew Archer, Melanie Leather,
Liz Marcy, Matthew Packer, Victoria Prior and Marcus Waring
Sub editors: Camilla Doodson and Richard Rees

The right of the author to be identified as the author of this work has been asserted by him/her/them in accordance with the Copyright, Designs and Patents Act 1988. All rights reserved. No part of this publication may be reproduced, stored in or introduced into a retrieval system, or transmitted, in any form, or by any means (electronic, mechanical, photocopying, recording or otherwise) without the prior written permission of the publisher. Any person who does any unauthorised act in relation to this publication may be liable to criminal prosecution and civil claims for damages.

1 3 5 7 9 8 6 4 2 1

A CIP catalogue record for this book is available from the British Library.

Printed in Italy by Printer Trento S.r.l

Visit www.panmacmillan.com to read more about all our books and to buy them.
You will also find features, author interviews and news of any author events, and you can sign up
for e-newsletters so that you're always first to hear about our new releases.

Cover image: JP Greenwood / Getty

THANKS

The authors and the Think Books team would like to thank all the restaurant chefs, owners and PR representatives for time given when researching this book.

In particular:

Hayley Abbot, Rachel Argyle, Véronique Bras, Mark Collins, Karima Dubois, Jean-Louis Faury, Christian Giles, Agneta Green, Yohann Herman, Ryzlène Jaïdi, Akiko Julien, Eleanor Kerwan, Inken Kipker, Peter Kreiner, David López, Betina von Massenbach, Benoit Massonneau, Rita Matar, Sanne Mooij, Susana Nieto Muñoz, Mandy Oser, René Redzepi, Christophe Rohat, Julia Ruttner, Jessica Salmon, Antonio, Giovanni and Nadia Santini, Romina Savi, Sarah Swan, Alessandro Tomberli, Eugenia Trotta, Kirsty Tyrrell, Hans Välimäki, Sally Wood and Tamara K Wood.

For their support, advice and insightful knowledge, we'd also like to thank Andrew Archer, Russell Dodd, Karin Mueller and Victoria Prior at William Reed and *Restaurant* magazine.

For additional research: Ben Ashwell, Aaron Biddle, Beatrice Carvalho and Ben Whittacker-Cook.

FOREWORD

For three years in a row (four if you count 2002), this award has judged my restaurant to be the best in the world so, as you can expect, it's quite difficult for me to take a dispassionate assessment of its relevance and interest. And yet, every year, I find it incredible that I have won. I know that in future lists it may be other restaurants that take the top spot. It couldn't be any other way.

Like all lists, the The S.Pellegrino World's 50 Best Restaurants has its controversial aspects. No award can escape being the target of objections: even the Oscars and Nobel Prizes occasion an annual polemic. Nevertheless, there are many aspects of the list that cannot be ignored. First, it has meant that haute cuisine has been opened up to the whole world, spreading beyond its former boundaries, which saw it centred exclusively on half a dozen countries in Western Europe. It has, for example, helped put the US on the gastronomic map, as well as other countries in South America and Australasia. It has also played its part in the growing recognition of Asia's gastronomic heritage – a territory that has traditionally been little understood due to cultural, particularly linguistic, differences.

And, as with all projects, there is no doubt that this list will continue to evolve and improve. There have already been a number of changes for the better, such as the introduction in 2006 of a new judging system that results in great objectivity, as it hinges on the votes of some 700 professionals within the sector. I firmly believe that this group's opinion can be considered much more reliable than that of a smaller panel of judges.

For me, the The S.Pellegrino World's 50 Best Restaurants list inspires nothing but positive benefits. The prize-giving ceremony organised each year in London is a great excuse, the best of occasions, for us to meet up with colleagues. And each year I think the same thing: that, as a general rule, we are a community where there is mutual respect and admiration, where new techniques and discoveries are shared. I'm sure that very few disciplines can boast of such unity, such diversity of styles and of such respect for the work of others. Proof of this lies in the fact that when El Bulli was awarded the accolade of best restaurant, I immediately received messages of congratulation from others on the list. There could be no more attractive symbol of an initiative that is currently reaching new heights and whose vitality and interest increases year by year.

Ferran Adrià, El Bulli, June 2008

INTRODUCTION

There's nothing like a list for generating debate, and all 50 restaurants on this one will have their detractors as well as their ardent fans. But there's one thing that all of the restaurants have in common; a genuine, heart-felt wish to show their guests the best time possible. Some do this with a certain amount of pomp and ceremony; others take a more relaxed approach. Some restaurants are part of what seem to be global corporations, while others are owned and run by generations of the same family. Some soothe the soul while others agitate with edgy theatricality. Some of them are eye-wateringly expensive while others are… well, merely expensive. But no restaurant on this list is the exclusive preserve of oligarchs and plutocrats, and all of the chefs and restaurateurs I spoke to when compiling this book talked about the joy they felt in being able to share their passion and enthusiasm with people for whom fine dining was not an everyday event. The restaurant business has now captured the popular imagination to the extent that it is the stuff of prime-time television, and this means that enthusiasts are arguably just as likely to save up for a meal at a special restaurant as they are for tickets to a once-in-a-lifetime sports fixture or concert. Come one, come all. Chefs and restaurateurs are by their very nature hospitable and generous people, who love to welcome open-minded diners eager to broaden their culinary horizons.

Many of the chefs on this list would be considered artists or visionaries, reinventing dishes to create multi-sensory experiences that challenge our preconceptions of what food is or should be. Others are creating new dining paradigms, even to the point of having to invent new presentational devices to showcase their offerings (knives, forks and plates just don't have what it takes any more). And some people have little patience for what they see as smoke-and-mirrors trickery, designed to part fools and their money. It's just food, isn't it? Well, of course, in the end, yes. And Picasso would have done a beautiful job painting your skirting boards. But in our post-modern age, the culinary arts have taken their place with other ostensibly non-essential but ultimately life-affirming forms of human endeavour that help shape long-lasting memories, make the world a more beautiful place and help us make sense of… well, everything. Clearly, food can touch the soul as much as any music or artwork could, and more than one chef I spoke to mentioned customers who ate with tears of joy running down their faces. As journalist AJ Liebling pointed out, 'In the light of what Proust wrote with so mild a stimulus, it is the world's loss that he did not have a heartier appetite.'

Liz Marcy (co-author), July 2008

Tempura pheasant, cider and shallot served on an oak branch with smoldering leaves, by Grant Achatz of Alinea restaurant, Chicago (p94)

THE JUDGING ACADEMY

The S.Pellegrino World's 50 Best Restaurants started small. In 2002, *Restaurant* magazine, the London-based hospitality industry bible, then just a year old, compiled the inaugural list from a comparatively informal survey of leading restaurant industry figures. That first ad hoc list made headlines the world over. Every year since then, the list's influence has grown exponentially, and its publication every April is now accompanied by an increasingly loud and increasingly public debate about the state of the global restaurant industry. Today the list is recognised as the most credible indicator of the best places to eat and drink on the planet.

How the voting works

2006 was the fifth year of the '50 Best' and a turning point in the event's history. It was in that year that the voting system was formalised in response to the list's ever-growing power and responsibility – and the vocal criticism that goes hand-in-hand with such power. An 'academy' style voting system was thus introduced to make the hotly-contested list more transparent and more authoritative than ever before. This academy is now known as the Nespresso World's 50 Best Restaurants Academy.

For the S.Pellegrino World's 50 Best Restaurants 2008, we divvied up the world into 23 voting regions, and for each one we appointed a chairperson. The chairperson, as you'll see from the list opposite, is a well-informed, well-travelled and well-regarded gourmand with a good, healthy (or not so healthy) appetite. They are prominent critics, commentators, food writers and publishers, the very mention of whose names has chefs quaking in their boots.

Each chair is tasked with the annual selection of an authoritative panel of (usually 31) experts (chefs, restaurateurs, critics and writers) in their region. These panel members in turn each get five votes. In 2008, the number of judges invited to vote was 682. Do the maths and you'll see that's an impressive 3,410 votes.

There are some conditions attached. Voters can only vote for two venues from within their own region; they must have eaten at all five of their chosen restaurants in the last 18 months; and in the case of the chefs and restaurateurs, they can't vote for themselves (though some do try…). In the event of two restaurants being tied with the same number of votes, the votes from their home region are discounted. If that still doesn't settle matters, preference is given to the restaurant that has votes spread across the largest number of regions.

All 3,410 votes are confidential. The voters, never named until after publication, place their votes on a specially created website. There's no list of nominees. So if voters want to single out a beach hut on Phuket, a 'mom and pop' joint in the Deep South or an extravagant temple to haute gastronomie in Paris, they may do. Each year, the panel's shaken up again, with about 30 per cent passing on the baton to new voters. Thus no elite 'club' of voters will ever be formed, and we can ensure we're reflecting the voices of the many, not the few. The academy and voting regions are reassessed every year to ensure that they are truly reflective of the global industry and the relative strength of the regions' restaurant scenes.

Chefs often ask: 'How do I get my restaurant on the list?' We don't have the answer to that. Publishing the above is as close as we get. The best people to ask are the previous winners, Ferran Adrià, Thomas Keller and Heston Blumenthal. But if they know the secret, they're not letting on.

Hilary Armstrong
Consultant to The S.Pellegrino World's 50 Best Restaurants

The Nespresso World's 50 Best Restaurants Academy 2008

UK & Ireland Jay Rayner, restaurant critic and food writer, *The Observer*, *31 voters*

France François Simon, restaurant critic, *Le Figaro*, *31 voters*

Spain & Portugal Rafael Anson, president of the Spanish Academy of Gastronomy, *31 voters*

Italy Andrea Petrini, food and travel writer, *31 voters*

Germany Jörg Leu, marketing manager, *Schlemmer Atlas*, *31 voters*

Austria, Switzerland & Liechtenstein Hannes Konzett, editor-in-chief, *Oscar's Hotel and Restaurant Magazine*, *31 voters*

Greece, Turkey, Cyprus & Georgia Dimitris Antonopoulos, editor and wine critic, *Athinorama Magazine*, *31 voters*

Benelux Dirk de Prins, editor, *Ambiance Magazine*, *31 voters*

Denmark, Sweden & Norway Jan Nilsson, editor-in-chief, *Gourmet Magazine*, Sweden, *31 voters*

NE Europe, Iceland & Greenland Kenneth Nars, restaurant critic, *Hufvudstadsbladet*, Finland, *31 voters*

Eastern Europe Bianca Otero, visual/content editor, *The Dining Guide & Where Magazine*, Hungary, *31 voters*

Central Asia & Russia Andrey Zakharin, editor-in-chief, *Gastronom*, Russia, *31 voters*

South East Asia Leisa Tyler, food and travel writer and photographer, *31 voters*

India & Subcontinent Rashmi Uday Singh, food writer and broadcaster, *31 voters*

Japan & Korea Yumiko Inukai, restaurant writer, *31 voters*

China, HK & Taiwan Grant Thatcher, founder and publishing editor, the *LUXE City Guides*, *31 voters*

North America Steve Dolinsky, food/lifestyle reporter, *ABC 7*, Chicago, *31 voters*

Central America & Mexico Jorge Toledo Y Leyva, restaurant critic, *El Economista*, Mexico, *16 voters*

South America Josimar Melo, food critic, *Folha de S.Paolo*, Brazil, *31 voters*

Caribbean & Bahamas Wendy Knight, travel writer *15 voters*

Middle East & North Africa Lisa Magloff, journalist, writer and editor, *31 voters*

Southern Africa Lannice Snyman, publisher, *31 voters*

Australasia & Oceania Pat Nourse, features editor, *Australian Gourmet Traveller*, *31 voters*

AWARD SPONSORS

S.Pellegrino, one of the longest-established sparkling mineral waters in the world, has been an intrinsic part of Italian life since 1899. First discovered in the 13th century, the spring is located in the foothills of the Alps, close to Bergamo, Italy. S.Pellegrino water is characterised by its naturally light carbonation and balanced composition of mineral salts, while its still-water counterpart *Acqua Panna*, which hails from Tuscany, has a light, soft taste and a low sodium content. Both brands are lauded by chefs and sommeliers around the world as the perfect compliment to fine dining.

Nespresso is proud to sponsor the World's 50 Best Restaurants, underlining our commitment to high-end gastronomy. Our non-stop quest for quality extends into every stage of the journey that transforms green coffee into the perfect Nespresso Grand Cru – with the exquisite aroma and full-bodied taste that truly sets Nespresso coffee apart.

Established in 1812, *Laurent-Perrier* is one of the most distinguished family-owned champagne houses. Renowned for crafting a diverse and pioneering range of champagnes, from the prestigious multi-vintage Grand Siècle to the unequalled Cuvée Rosé Brut, Laurent-Perrier enjoys a reputation as an artisan of exceptional quality and taste.

Alliance acts for many top names in the fine-dining market, understanding the needs of restaurant entrepreneurs and business leaders. We offer wide-ranging insurance together with support in

health and safety, food hygiene, disaster recovery planning and other areas of risk management. Our ultimate focus is your brand protection.

American Express is proud to once again sponsor the World's 50 Best Restaurants awards. American Express also strives to be a valuable business partner by helping drive revenue to restaurants. Through unique partnerships, we can provide restaurateurs with opportunities to market exclusive offers directly to our higher-spending card members.

Since 1998, *Eureka Executive Search* has been providing the most process-driven executive, management and specialist talent-hunting service to the hospitality and retail industries. Our strategy relies on supporting the leaders in their fields, in industries we understand, throughout the world's most dynamic markets via our offices in London and Paris.

Electrolux Professional-Foodservice offers a complete solution to your kitchen environment for the production and distribution of professional foodservice solutions, from storage and preparation to cooking and dishwashing.

As a leading international supplier of innovative and inspirational tableware, *Steelite International* is delighted to sponsor 50 Best, which recognises excellence in this global industry. Steelite International is world renowned for its complete tabletop solutions, from stunning flatware and service items to fine stemware and cutlery.

HOW TO USE THIS BOOK

The S. Pellegrino World's 50 Best Restaurants Awards is recognised by chefs and diners as the world's most credible indicator of the best places to eat, but this is the first year that the winners have been celebrated in book form.

However, *S. Pellegrino World's 50 Best Restaurants* hasn't just been created to acknowledge the winner's culinary expertise; this book has also been put together to provide readers and gourmands with the inspiration and information they need to book, visit and dine in these fabulous venues.

And that's why we haven't just stuck to the top 50 winners. Every year, the Nespresso World's 50 Best Academy creates a shortlist of the top 100 restaurants worldwide and, although not all make it into the top 50, they all deserve to be recognised – and visited – for their culinary skill.

The restaurants are all different in style and location: some can be found on the streets of our capital cities; others exist in the most remote locations. Some form part of a global chain of restaurants or encapsulate a modern food trend (see the glossary of terms, right), while others are family-run and deeply traditional. The cost of dining can vary drastically, too, as can the relative sophistication of the décor and the welcome. What does not vary, however, is the quality of the food.

Glossary of terms

You will see the following categories and terms used frequently in the *S. Pellegrino World's 50 Best Restaurants*; for specific information by restaurant, please refer to the individual entries.

Approximate cost for two: The average cost for two diners at the time of press, including set menu costs (whether seasonal, tasting or lunch) and wine, where appropriate.

Gault Millau: One of France's most influential restaurant guides, *Gault Millau* has its own rating system that awards restaurants points on a scale of 1-20. Unlike the *Michelin Restaurant Guide*, points are awarded based solely on the quality of the food, with any comments about service, price or the atmosphere of the restaurant given separately.

Head chef: Although many of these restaurants are most commonly associated with a celebrity backer, restaurateur or TV chef, there are also many lesser-known chefs who work tirelessly behind the stoves in order to produce the quality that has led to their status on the S.Pellegrino World's 50 Best Restaurants list. Where possible, we have credited each chef as chef-owner, chef-restaurateur, head chef or executive chef.

On the menu: Some restaurants have signature dishes that remain on the menu throughout the career of the chef; others have menus that change seasonally or daily to reflect the area's seasonal produce and the desire of the chef to make the best use of it. In order to guide the reader, we have highlighted a mixture of signature dishes, new additions to the menu and old favourites.

Michelin stars: Of the thousands of restaurants the *Michelin Restaurant Guide* mentions, only a limited number are awarded the coveted stars. The guide was originally created to accompany road touring, so the stars relate to the relative merit of stopping off en-route: one star means restaurants are worth visiting if they're on the way; two means they're worth a detour; and three means they're worth a special trip by themselves.

Molecular gastronomy: A term most widely associated with the chefs of Spain's Basque country, as well as Heston Blumenthal and others in the UK; few chefs these days accept the categorisation of molecular gastronomy. At its essence, the term refers to a highly evolved style of cooking that combines culinary skill with scientific method. For example, the attempt to find the proper ratio of potato and cooking fat to make the perfect chip.

'La piedra pomez' (the pumice stone) at Arzak (p46)

Techno-emotional: A new buzzword amongst French and Spanish chefs, this refers to the application of technological advances to culinary expertise in order to produce an emotional reaction by the diner.

Top tips: Look here for tips on how to book, where to stay, what to ask for and how to get there. Look to the 'Did you know?' section for insights on the chefs, the venues and the restaurants.

Every attempt has been made to ensure that this is information is correct at the time of press; however, in an industry as fast-paced as the restaurant industry, menus and dishes can change frequently – sometimes daily. Where possible, we have endeavoured to feature each restaurant's most popular or current signature dishes, but if you have any specific requests, please check with the restaurant before you book to avoid disappointment. Enjoy!

THE
S.PELLEGRINO
WORLD'S
50
BEST
RESTAURANTS

POSITIONS 1 TO 50

EL BULLI

El Bulli is a restaurant that really gets people talking. Is it food? Is this 'dining'? If I eat at El Bulli am I truly a 'consumer' of art? Or a consumer of 'art'? Ferran Adrià is the genius behind this restaurant, located on the rocky Costa Brava in Spain, with splendid views over the Mediterranean making up for the oddly nondescript décor. But nobody's here for the décor or the scenery, they're here to sample Adrià's ingenious, evolved cuisine, which has made him the toast of the gastronomic world. The food plays with expectations, draws on long-forgotten taste memories and involves all the senses; temperature, texture, smell and taste are Adrià's playthings, his playground the 30-odd-course tasting menu served to each customer (the restaurant will ask you if you have any strong dislikes or dietary restrictions at the time of booking). Menu descriptions are brief to the point of being terse, and in any event can't prepare one for what you're likely to get. A 'tortilla Espanol' in a sherry glass, for example, into which one is urged to dig deep to commingle flavours of potato (delivered as a foam), essence of rich, sweet onion and creamy egg sabayon; or the Catalan staple tomato bread, which comes in the form of a cloud of bread

El Bulli

'In El Bulli we don't only look to feed people well, but also to provoke new sensations of all kinds: intellectual, emotional, for the palate. We push the limits of creativity in the kitchen and we like to share this with our clients'

filled with warm olive oil, served on a tomato sorbet. Some, like the 'Kellogg's paella' (crisped rice with a rich fish broth) are humorous and are greeted with giggles of delight. Others awe diners into silence, but the delightful parade is paced to entertain and inspire, starting with a flight of appetisers, moving on to tapas-sized portions eaten with a spoon, and ending with desserts. In spite of the sheer number of courses, diners often report feeling refreshed after four or five-hour meals that can start in the early evening on the terrace and end well after midnight.

The restaurant seats only 50, is open only between April and October, only for dinner. Oh, and it's closed on Mondays and Tuesdays. So, in all, there are only opportunities for about 8,000 diners a season, while around half a million will apply, by email, from mid-October the previous year. Diners can wait months before they find out whether or not they've been successful. But those who do score reservations don't mind, and duly make their travel arrangements, wending their way up the winding road to culinary nirvana on the appointed date.

Adrià admits that the restaurant hasn't really made any money since they stopped the lunch service. Given that the restaurant turns away thousands of diners every season, he's aware he could use the laws of supply and demand and double or triple the amount he charges, but doesn't want El Bulli simply to be a restaurant for the rich. As it is, he is cognisant of the fact that many of his clients come a long way, a big motivation for seeking to be innovative. 'In El Bulli we don't only look to feed people well, but also to provoke new sensations of all kinds: intellectual, emotional, for the palate. We push the limits of creativity in the kitchen and we like to share this with our clients.' As long as Adrià is working, he'll be creating, and as long as he's creating people will be talking about it.

ON ORDER

Cala Montjoi, 17480 Roses, Girona, Spain

+34 972 150 457; www.elbulli.com

Head chef: *Ferran Adrià*

On the menu: *Cocktails, dry snacks and fresh snacks for the first 'act'; savory dishes for the second; desserts for the third, and coffee and 'morphings' for the fourth and final act*

Did you know? *Luis Garcia is the man charged with allocating reservations. He does this following strict criteria: 50 per cent of guests have never eaten at El Bulli before (50 per cent are returning guests) and 50 per cent are Spanish (the rest made up by diners from overseas)*

Top tip: *If you are lucky enough to get a reservation, don't try and pass it on to someone else or you'll be blacklisted*

Approximate cost for two: *The 2008 tasting menu is €430 for two, drinks and VAT not included*

The life and work of Ferran Adrià

Ferran Adrià was born in 1962 in a suburb of Barcelona. His father was a house painter, and Adrià was more interested in football than in food – in fact, he got his first job in a kitchen in 1980 so that he could go to Ibiza and meet girls. He worked in various kitchens until he started his military service in the navy in 1982, becoming part of the Admiral's kitchen staff. While he was there a friend suggested that they should spend their month-long leave in the kitchens of a restaurant he'd heard of on the Costa Brava: El Bulli. This they did, and it impressed Adrià (and vice versa) to the extent that he decided to join the restaurant staff permanently when his military service was over the following year.

The same year Adrià started permanently at the restaurant, the chef announced he was leaving, so in October 1984, Adrià and Christian Lutaud became joint chefs de cuisine. A slow winter season gave the pair the opportunity to regroup and visit other restaurants, as a result of which arrangements were made for the pair to undertake in-service traineeships, Adrià at Georges Blanc and Jacques Pic, and Lutaud with Troisgros and Michel Chabran, which they completed in 1985. That same year, Adrià's brother Albert Adrià arrived, aged just 15. He ended up specialising in pastry quite by chance. As well as having a natural aptitude, a hereditary allergy to shellfish made it difficult for him to work in other parts of the kitchen.

Christian Lutaud left El Bulli to open a restaurant in Alicante in 1987, just as Adrià was starting to become more serious about his vocation. He was happy to take over completely and decide what direction the kitchen should take. That same year, he happened to be present at a demonstration by chef Jacques Maximin of the Chantecler in Nice. During the discussion afterwards, someone asked him what creativity was. Maximin replied: 'Creativity means not copying'. This resulted in a complete change of direction for Adrià, who decided he'd no longer recreate what others had done, but would be a creator instead.

'To be anarchic, you have to be organised'

In 1990, the owners of El Bulli retired and sold the restaurant to manager Juli Soler and Adrià. The pair made alterations that included a new kitchen and a 'workshop' in Barcelona dedicated to creativity. This in 2003 spawned a science department to investigate the new textures they had been creating. 'We decided to find out why these preparations were possible, what physical and chemical processes were involved and how the products that made these textures possible acted.'

In spite of this interest in scientific process, Adrià is resistant to the idea that he practises 'molecular gastronomy'. His interest in the scientific process can perhaps be better read as part of his over-arching interest in documenting his evolution as a cook. 'To be anarchic, you have to be organised,' he says. Thus in 2000, work started on the El Bulli general catalogue: dating and numbering all creations. He can say with certainty that he first used a whipped cream siphon in 1994; that dishes involving hot jellies emerged in 1998. But Adrià believes such creations have been part of a purely culinary quest. He asserts that: 'The public should not be tricked into believing that molecular cuisine is a cooking style. If a chef wants to label his work as molecular cuisine, he is at liberty to do so. But in the name of that liberty, I claim to be merely a cook; and everything we do at El Bulli as cooking.'

THE FAT DUCK

Heston Blumenthal's inimitable and charming culinary wizardry gleefully engages all the senses. His restaurant, The Fat Duck, is in Bray, a village west of London. It serves 40 diners at a time, multi-course tasting menus that confound and delight the senses. His dishes have become legendary: the 'sound of the sea' – a seaweed and seafood combination served as if washed up by shellfish foam on tapioca 'sand' with an iPod playing the sound of waves; the orange and beetroot jelly surprise; the Nitro scrambled egg and smoked bacon ice-cream; the snail porridge. These dishes have become classics, but have been joined by a parallel tasting menu of dishes inspired by historic British dishes. 'We have such a rich tradition of food in this country,' he says. 'In the 18th century our food was the best in Europe – but these recipes have been dead and buried for years.'

Born in 1966 in London, Blumenthal experienced an epiphany at 15 when he went on holiday to the south of France. The family ate one night at the legendary Provençal restaurant L'Oustau de Baumanière, and from that moment Blumenthal realised that the gastronomic life was for him.

Why molecular gastronomy?

His is a highly evolved style of cooking that draws upon scientific method, but Blumenthal regrets the misconceptions that surround the term 'molecular gastronomy'. 'It's as much about frying an egg, roasting a chicken or making some chips. Understanding the cooking process can benefit all of these things in some way or another. I feel that in cooking, as in life, the more information you have about the way things work, the more enriching it is.' For him, it's a means to an end rather than the end in itself: 'The danger comes when new technologies, ideas and ingredients, completely take over the traditional approach and you get over-excited about the technological side of things, and forget about the dish itself – "It spins around, jumps up in the air and sings a funny song! Hooray, it's brilliant!... But does it taste good?" – People can get so excited about the new stuff that quality control goes out of the window.'

'I feel that in cooking, as in life, the more information you have about the way things work, the more enriching it is'

Almost immediately on his return to England he began teaching himself to cook, and for the next decade he gave over all of his spare time (really, says Blumenthal, it was every minute) to reading, learning, experimenting, cooking, travelling and researching.

A second epiphany occurred when he read Harold McGee's book *On Food and Cooking*, which challenged culinary shibboleths and encouraged chefs to question the preconceived notions of how and why certain cooking methods worked. Blumenthal feels this is where not being a classically trained chef came into its own: 'Because I didn't have that, I had the naivety to lose the boundaries in other areas, too. A classical, hierarchical education can make some chefs reluctant to try new things.'

Other than a couple of brief stages in other kitchens (including, for a week, Le Manoir aux Quat' Saisons, where he met and befriended Marco Pierre White), his first experience as a chef was when he opened The Fat Duck in 1995. He wouldn't recommend this approach to anybody. 'I had to work 20 hours a day, six days a week, plus cope with the pressure that came with trying to run a business. I had no idea whether I'd be able to cope with it or not. In hindsight I was lucky I could. It was naivety that got me there. The fear of failure was more of a drive than the will to succeed.'

It was only subsequently that he realised the L'Oustau de Baumanière experience had given him more than just a desire to cook. He remembers the sense of excitement and wonder, and this multi-sensory experience is what he's trying to give his customers today. 'One of the unique things about The Fat Duck is that it looks like a cramped 16th-century cottage. There's no view and it's on the side of the road. The memories I had in France were about all the things around me – I haven't got them here, so it's almost as if that's forced me to try and create them at the table.'

ON ORDER

High Street, Bray, Berkshire SL6 2AQ, UK

+44 (0)1628 580333; www.fatduck.co.uk

Head chef: *Heston Blumenthal and Ashley Palmer-Watts*

On the menu: *Snail porridge, 'sound of the sea' and mango and Douglas fir purée*

Did you know? *Heston Blumenthal worked as a debt collector and a photocopier salesman while he was teaching himself to cook*

Top tip: *Despite rumours that The Fat Duck is booked years in advance, the restaurant actually doesn't take bookings more than two months in advance. Phone with a choice of dates for the best chance of success*

Approximate cost for two: *Tasting menu is £125 each. Accompanying wine from £90 per person*

PIERRE GAGNAIRE

Pierre Gagnaire has been called a visionary, a poet, an artist and a magician. His dishes – free-form, deconstructed, composed of several elements that shouldn't work together but do, brilliantly – are individual works of art. 'My big revelation came when I discovered that I'm not a robotic person,' he says. I discovered I have a talent for composing notes and colours. I have a talent for conceiving tastes. It's not something dramatic, not some gastronomic revolution, I've just given a little twist to improve something. Like rock 'n' roll!' The musical analogy is apt; Gagnaire is a jazz aficionado. 'Discovering jazz was a big shock,' he says. 'It is like cooking, it has many forms and rhythms, like life. My cuisine imposes its own rhythm.'

He was born in 1950 in Apinac, west of Saint-Etienne, in the Rhône-Alpes region of France. His family was in the business – his father ran a restaurant called Clos Fleury that Gagnaire describes as 'a restaurant of weddings and banquets'. To begin with Gagnaire had no wish to be a chef. But he succumbed to the inevitable ('I had a tocque on my head when I was five years old,' he has said in the past) and started as a commis at 18 in the legendary Lyon restaurant

A magician's art

Though he stresses that 'all classics were once modern', Gagnaire's approach has been to free himself from the exigencies of 'classic' dishes and techniques. This means taking risks. His dishes are composed of elements that differ considerably in flavour and texture, so every time another one is added, he runs the risk of ruining the harmony of the dish. But he is interested above all in transformation: the way that a great dish is made by a subtle series of interactions. In order to understand some of these interactions he's teamed up with Hervé This, a chemist at the College de France, who is considered the father of 'molecular cuisine'. But it would be reductive to think of the power of Gagnaire's cuisine as purely chemical. Gagnaire also considers it to be emotional: it takes place both in the pan and on the plate, in the heads and, perhaps most of all, in the hearts of the people who make the pilgrimage to the rue Balzac.

'Gastronomy gives you access to another universe. You touch people, you touch their hearts. I've seen people cry sitting at the table'

Tante Alice, cooking quenelles and chicken 'demi-deuil' (with truffles under the skin). From there he cooked in various grand restaurants, as well as, for two years, in the navy, before travelling the world for a couple of years and finally, in 1976, returning to the Clos Fleury to cook. He says of this period, and the years immediately following: 'I worked for 10 years in different restaurants. Always the same produce, no emotion. I learned a little technique, but the French cuisine I learned was at a dead end.'

In 1980 he went solo and opened a restaurant of his own in Saint-Etienne. During this era he cooked for heads of state at the behest of President François Mitterrand. But he was forced to concede, in 1996, that the gamble he had made by opening a restaurant in industrial Saint-Etienne, where there were no tourists, and not enough money (or interest) for top-level cuisine, had not paid off. For the first time in the history of the Michelin Guide, an establishment endowed with the maximum number of stars went bankrupt.

Not daunted, Gagnaire moved instead to Paris, where he found a home at the Hotel Balzac, near the Arc de Triomphe, and a public open to his brand of associative, instinctive and emotional cooking. The interior is sober, harmonious, comfortable. A pale wood and pearl-grey colour scheme, flowers and soft lighting create a refined and calm atmosphere that is described as being 'a favourable climate for communing with the dishes'.

Gagnaire intends the experience of eating his food to be transcendent, transformative: 'Gastronomy gives you access to another universe. You touch people, you touch their hearts. I've seen people cry sitting at the table. I need to position my cuisine visually. I follow my instinct, which helps me determine qualities and flaws, and sometimes new flavours I was unaware of.'

ON ORDER

6 rue Balzac, 75008 Paris, France

+33 (0)1 5836 1250; www.pierre-gagnaire.com

Head chef: *Pierre Gagnaire and second chef Michel Nave*

On the menu: *'Le Printemps' (spring), côte de veau de lait rôtie entière au plat; and grenouilles meunière enrobées d'une fine polenta au colombo*

Did you know? *Pierre Gagnaire and chemist Hervé This are working together to unite science and cuisine. You can find out about their latest experiments with food science on www.pierre-gagnaire.com*

Top tip: *If you can't get a table at Pierre Gagnaire, Gagnaire's Left Bank seafood restaurant Gaya is easier to book, not to mention much cheaper*

Approximate cost for two: *The fixed-price Menu du Marché is €210 for two, not including wine. The degustation menu is €510 for two, again not including wine. The average cost of the à la carte menu is €300. Wine starts at €60*

MUGARITZ

Andoni Luis Aduriz is often portrayed as the quiet man of the Spanish cooking scene. His food is less flamboyant than that of many modern Spanish chefs, and, ostensibly, he is less driven by new technology and kitchen science. But it is all a matter of degree. Aduriz famously spent two years studying the chemistry of coagulation in order to produce the perfect poached egg.

His culinary expertise relies on immaculate technical precision accumulated during nine years at cookery school, followed by stints in seven restaurant kitchens, including two years at both Zuberoa and El Bulli. He has been called a variously a 'gastronomic genius' and 'the poet' of Spanish cuisine, and was awarded the National Gastronomy Prize of Spain in 2002 when he was in possession of his first Michelin star. His second came a little later in 2005.

But while Aduriz may be associated with the molecular gastronomy movement, the learning and technical wizardry that drives it very much plays a supporting role in the Mugaritz kitchen. For him it is the combination of technology and emotion that drives his technique and his ultimate goal: the

Delectable desserts

Mugaritz offers a choice between two tasting menus (one at €95 and one at €125), but both include sumptuous desserts, presented in Aduriz's distinctive fashion. At present, guests can choose from his 'interpretation of vanity' (moist chocolate cake, cold almond cream, 'bubbles' and cocoa) or 'the contrast of temperatures, textures and cultures' that exists in his violet ice cream, hot almond marzipan, shaving of spiced bread and green tea. And if that all sounds too rich, why not go for the crunchy milk sheets with confit of kidney beans?

Each meal is served with measured deliberation, allowing guests not only to soak up the flavours, but also to settle into Mugaritz's warm and homely atmosphere

creation of dishes that tantalise not only the palate, but also the senses. Journalist Pau Arenós coined a word to define Mugaritz´s cuisine: 'techno-emotion'.

This emotion is created not simply by the dishes, but also the setting and pace with which his food is served. Each meal (a choice of two tasting menus) is served with measured deliberation, allowing guests to soak up the flavours and settle into Mugaritz's warm and homely atmosphere. So measured is the service that late diners must restrict themselves to only six dishes in order to avoid rushing the experience.

From the exterior, the restaurant's rustic décor and lovingly tended kitchen herb garden seem worlds away from the high-end presentation of his food, but for Aduriz, it is all about the raw ingredient. His menus play creative homage to the natural world, emphasising the flavour and goodness of the ingredients he finds on his doorstep. It has, at times, been called pretentious, but this subtle and earthy approach has resulted in some of his most successful dishes: warm lettuce hearts soaked in vanilla brine; sheep's milk curd seasoned with hay and toasted fern; beef roasted with the embers of vine cuttings.

Aduriz loves to explore obscure ingredients, such as dandelion petals, roasted acorn skins or amaranth grains, but there are also more traditional choices on his menus; particularly those that reflect the culinary heritage of Spain's Basque country. So passionate is he, in fact, about the raw ingredients that can be found here that he also teaches a course at the University of the Basque Country that promotes creativity and innovation in the area's cuisine. Although that is not to say it's something the Basque country doesn't already have in abundance: its capital San Sebastián has the most Michelin stars per capita in the world and Mugaritz well deserves its place among them.

ON ORDER

Otzazulueta Baserria, Aldura Aldea 20, 20100 Errenteria Gipuzkoa, Spain

+34 943 522 455; www.mugaritz.com

Head chef: *Andoni Luis Aduriz*

On the menu: *What Aduriz describes as an 'essay of salads': warm lettuce hearts soaked in vanilla brine, a dressing of balsamic vinegar and country milk skins*

Did you know? *Aduriz once had to retake a year at catering college*

Top tip: *Arrive early to enjoy an aperitif on the outside terrace*

Approximate cost for two: *€300, not including wine*

THE FRENCH LAUNDRY

Thomas Keller took over The French Laundry in Yountville, in California's charming and bountiful Napa Valley, in 1994. The restaurant was already well established, having been run by a local family since 1974. Even the name was in place: in the early 20th century, the building had been a working laundry run by a French couple and the name stuck.

'The French Laundry was a complete accident,' says Keller. 'I was visiting a friend in Napa and he told me it was for sale. I explored it and, of course, immediately fell in love and was eventually able to buy it.' Though the first night was reputedly a disaster, it quickly became clear that this was a restaurant with serious intent, and recognition from the critics soon followed.

It wasn't Thomas Keller's first attempt at running a top-end restaurant. His New York restaurant, Rakel, had fallen victim to the economic downturn of the late 1980s, and Keller had relocated back to the West Coast (he's a California native). He later said of the

The personality of cuisine

Thomas Keller has referred to the kind of food that he prepares as 'personality cuisine' – hard to define using conventional terms but honed over many years by training, background and long-held beliefs. He says his personality makes him lean towards a cuisine that is predominantly rooted in the traditions of French cooking, citing the French chef Fernand Point as a major influence – his *Ma Gastronomie* is apparently almost required reading for anybody aspiring to work in a Keller kitchen. But at the same time his food is robustly produce-driven. He's a vocal advocate of small, artisanal producers and makes much of the local produce in the abundant Napa Valley, and this makes his cooking resolutely American.

'Food has reference points,' says Keller. 'Emotional reference points that really touch you and bring wonderful memories to the surface.' Dishes such as 'coffee and donuts', that create archetypes of what such dishes can aspire to be. Or 'peas and carrots' that distills the essence of these workaday vegetables and give them the capacity to surprise and elate.

He's careful when asked how he gets inspiration for his dishes: 'You can't really say what's going to inspire you in the future, though you can tell stories about things that have inspired you in the past.' His legendary dish of 'oysters and pearls' – poached oysters in a tapioca sauce topped with Osetra caviar – came from a trip to the supermarket. 'I saw a purple box with the word "pearls" on it, and it just happened to be tapioca. I thought to myself: "Where do pearls come from? Oysters." And that was the beginning of that dish.'

'Food has emotional reference points that can really touch you and bring wonderful memories to the surface'

experience: 'When you start service in a restaurant you have your *mise en place* – everything you'll need for a successful service. I knew how to do that as a cook, but I didn't know how to set up a restaurant.' But in typical style he made it a learning experience: 'I learned that I didn't know a lot about the service and financial sides, so I vowed that when I opened The French Laundry I would have people in place who had the knowledge and the commitment in those areas that I had in the kitchen. It was that base, that foundation, that made the restaurant such a success.'

Now, almost 15 years later, tables at The French Laundry are highly sought after. A strict policy means bookings are available precisely two months ahead of the required dates. Some have pointed out that this is a good thing, as it's about how long it takes to recover from the emotional trauma of continual redialling, without guarantee of success. All of this, however, adds to the mood of excited anticipation as diners arrive and are greeted by impeccably trained and attired waiting staff. The service style is a cornerstone of the French Laundry philosophy. Formal, but not stiff; proper, but flexible enough to place the diner at the centre of the experience; friendly but not: 'Hi, I'm David and I'll be your waiter tonight…'

There's no à la carte menu available; diners simply choose whether they want the chef's tasting menu or a vegetarian alternative, and wait. A succession of small dishes is then brought, each one as perfect as the last. The law of diminishing returns dictates that when one eats a large plate of food, each successive mouthful is enjoyed less. Keller aims to eliminate that sensation, by continually surprising the senses with a new dish, leaving the eater wishing for just one more bite.

ON ORDER

6640 Washington Street, Yountville, California 94599, USA

+1 (1) 707 944 2380; www.frenchlaundry.com

Head chef: *Thomas Keller and Corey Lee*

On the menu: *Cornet of salmon; calotte de bœuf*

Did you know? *Thomas Keller consulted on the film* Ratatouille, *about a loveable rat who's also a talented chef*

Top tip: *The restaurant takes bookings exactly two months ahead of time. Start calling at 10am local time and if you're lucky enough to get through, take anything you're offered – check if they have any cancellations before the date you're booking for*

Approximate cost for two: *Nine-course chef's or vegetable tasting menu, $240*

PER SE

Per Se is the East Coast urban 'interpretation' of Thomas Keller's California restaurant, The French Laundry. The two locations couldn't be more different. Where The French Laundry is a beacon of fine dining in laid-back Yountville, Per Se is located in the glitzy Time Warner Center near Central Park in nervy New York, surrounded by glamorous friends like Masa and Café Gray. 'It's at a wonderful height,' says Keller. 'You have a great sense of the city without being too far above it.'

But Keller hasn't really changed or compromised his basic philosophy, in spite of the radically different location. In fact, Keller went to extraordinary lengths to make sure he transferred and inculcated the French Laundry ethos into its new setting. First, he brought chef Jonathan Benno over to Yountville with the goal of training him up to run the new outpost, and familiarising him with house style, methods and recipes. He then took the unprecedented step of closing The French Laundry for five months and bringing the staff over to New York to prepare for the opening of Per Se. 'It's not just about the recipes, it's about the culture and philosophy,' he says. 'Once staff understand that, the

The story behind the blue aprons

According to French culinary tradition, white aprons are reserved for those who have ascended to the level of chef, having completed a journey that began as an apprentice wearing a blue apron. But within the kitchen of any Thomas Keller restaurant everyone, even the chef de cuisine, wears a blue apron during the hours prior to service, changing into white only once service begins.

While respect for tradition is a common thread among kitchen staff, what's just as important is the desire to constantly learn. Everything can always be done a little better. Everyone can always learn something new. It's that constant exploration that allows the experience to continually evolve. Assuming an apprentice's mindset for a little bit each day is a reminder of that, say the staff at Per Se.

'It's not just about the recipes, it's about the culture and philosphy'

rest falls into place. If they only know how to prepare and serve the food it's not going to work.'

Rumour has it that around $12 million was spent on creating the restaurant and its enormous kitchens – at 1,524 square metres, they're luxuriously appointed, especially in a city whose usual *modus operandi* is to maximise covers (ie profit) while dedicating the minimum amount of space behind the scenes. Here, the kitchens are almost as big as the dining room itself, and full of equipment designed to Keller's own specifications.

It all almost went disastrously wrong. In February 2004, when the restaurant had been open for just a few days, a small electrical fire broke out. Though the fire wasn't serious, there was considerable water and smoke damage, and one of the stoves had to be replaced. Keller – the perfectionist – delayed the reopening so that walls could be repainted and soft furnishings steam cleaned until all traces of the fire had been obliterated. The restaurant reopened in early May that year, leaving Keller just a few days before the scheduled reopening of The French Laundry.

'Obsessive' is a word Keller often uses about himself, and the rumour is that his kitchens are the most sterile any of his staff have ever seen, with not a thing out of place. Even the tape used to label everything is cut neatly, rather than hastily torn from the roll, because for Keller this is all part of the bigger picture; if this one thing is right then all will be right… and vice versa.

Anyone entering Per Se who has also visited The French Laundry will be greeted with familiar sights and symbols; the blue door, the olive garden and the earthy materials used in the dining room. It doesn't end there; the trademark salmon cornets begin each mealtime's parade of tiny dishes here just as they do 'back home'. And, luckily for Keller and his investors, reviewers have been reaching for the superlatives in the same way here as well.

ON ORDER

4th Floor, 10 Columbus Circle (at 60th Street), New York, NY 10019, USA

+ 1 (1) 212 823 9335; www.perseny.com

Head chefs: *Thomas Keller and Jonathan Benno*

On the menu: *'Oysters and pearls'; torchon of Moulard duck foie gras*

Did you know? *It's easier to book for lunch than dinner, and it's rumoured tables of four are preferred*

Top tip: *The food is split between two regularly changing nine-course menus – the chef's tasting menu and the seasonal 'tasting of vegetables' – both of which can disarm even the most cynical diners*

Approximate cost for two: *Five-course lunch menu, $175; nine-course vegetable tasting menu, $275; nine-course chef's tasting menu, $275*

BRAS

A 'seamless continuity', a 'modernism that grows naturally and instinctively out of the ancient' – that is the aim at Bras. And, if that sounds rather poetic, it's meant to. This isn't a restaurant that does anything as prosaic as merely feeding people, instead, it's an attempt to conjure the history, landscape and soul of this area of southern France in a series of thoughtful and engaging plates of food.

At first glance, Bras itself – a light-flooded glass, granite and slate ultra-modern structure jutting out of the hilltop – may not seem that pastoral. But the building, constructed in 1992, is deliberately intended to root staff and diners into the land. It was designed to mimic the stone peasant 'burons' that once littered the southern Auvernge region of France, and enjoys uninterrupted views of the surrounding countryside from its raised, panoramic lounge.

'The lifelong passion that I feel for this land gives me both profound knowledge and a capacity to capture the infinitesimal, the grandiose or the strange,' owner-chef Michel Bras says of the countryside in which he grew up. 'Whatever education and life may bring later on, every child has their native land in their

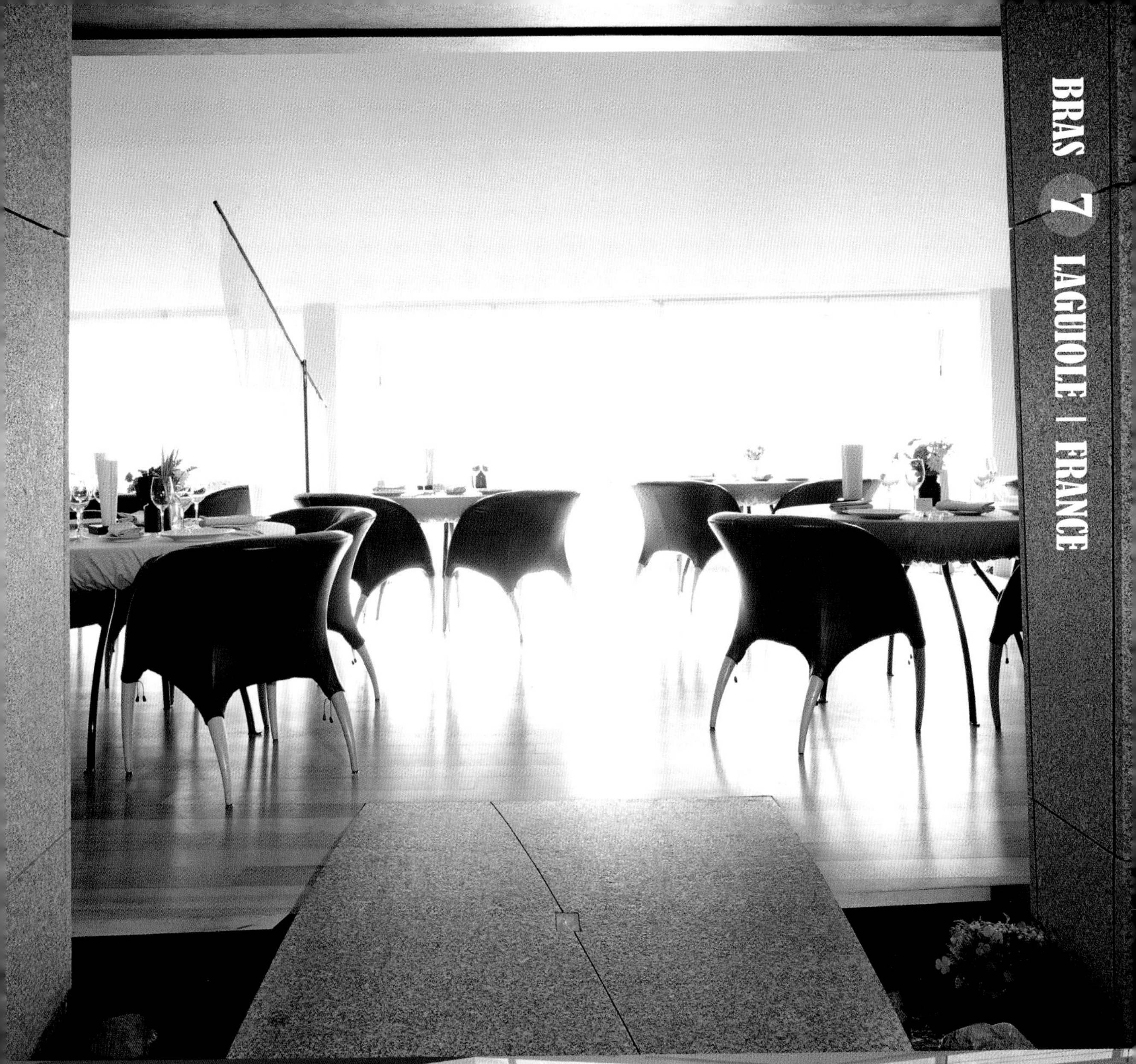

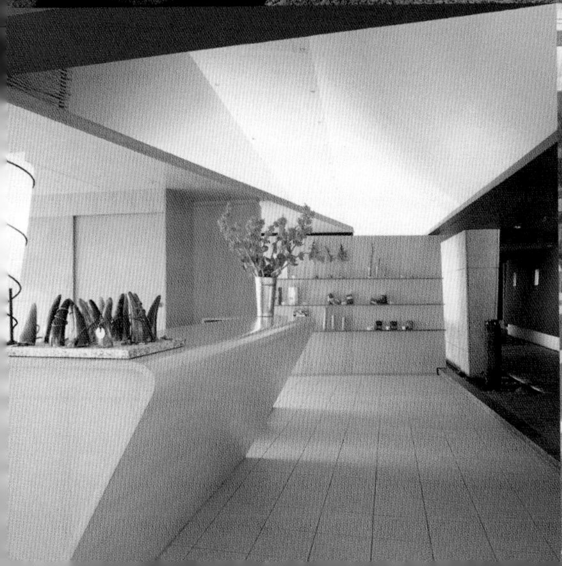

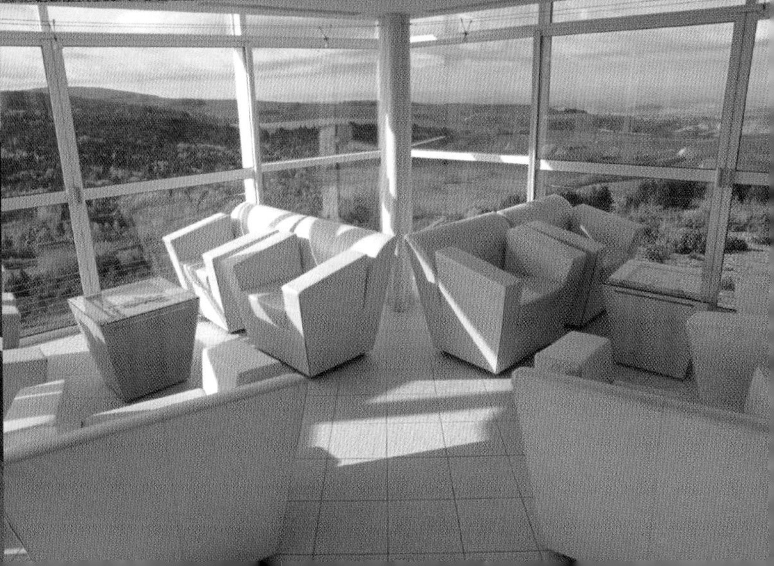

From the kitchen
Duck foie gras

- To prepare foie gras, you need to start four days in advance.
- The first day, soak the livers in salted, tepid water for about three hours. Separate the lobes and delicately remove the veins, being careful not to break them.
- Place the livers in a large dish and salt them evenly, using about 1½ tsp (7g) salt per 450g liver.
- Cover with plastic wrap and refrigerate for 24 hours.
- The following day, roast the livers in a cool oven, about 70°C, until they reach about 45°C in the centre. Once out of the oven, drain the excess fat from the roasting pan and let the livers cool for a few minutes.
- In an earthenware container, stack the liver pieces one on top of the other, smooth side up, the largest piece on the bottom, the smallest on top, the topmost piece smooth side down.
- Place a solid, flat object on top of the stacked pieces of foie gras to compress them. Weight the board with a heavy object.
- Refrigerate for 72 hours before serving.

Dishes are designed to insinuate a rusty autumn garden, or the winter light breaking through clouds

flesh, in their blood and in their conscience.' And it is that feeling, that harmony and that sense of nostalgia that he seeks to recreate in his kitchen.

In many ways it is a traditional family business. Father and son, Michel and Sébastien, cook. Mother Ginette and daughter-in-law Véronique provide the service, dressed in the restaurant's distinctive 'shepherd's smocks'. But this is a traditional family business producing food that even the most radical 'techno-emotional' chef would appreciate for the ambition and dexterity behind its creation. Dishes are designed to insinuate a rusty autumn garden, or the winter light breaking through clouds. One seeks to take you on a tour of the land, serving duck foie gras with peppered apple, beetroot and raspberries.

Bras' food doesn't just start on the plate, it starts with the plate: 'I choose a pure, white plate because I want nothing to distract from and conflict with the food,' he says. Like an artist, it is a blank canvas on which to create. Swirls of sauces are dabbed on with paint brushes, and petals from edible flowers and crushed seeds are positioned just so. The most famous is his 'gargouillou', which reinvents a peasant dish as an ever-changing, painstakingly assembled salad of 40 vegetables, flowers, herbs and seeds.

Bras rarely comes out of the kitchen, but his presence is felt everywhere: in the design of the room, the architecture of the building and the presentation of the food. It's modern but local with measured touches; the food is served with traditional Laguiole knives from the nearby town. Placed there to enrich the dining experience, not simply to profile and support the local industry. The menu constantly references the region and its heritage, serving ingredients that can't be found elsewhere, such as unpasteurised Laguiole cheese that is made in the traditional burons of which Michel is so fond.

ON ORDER

Route de l'Aubrac, 12 210 Laguiole, France

+33 (0)5 6551 1820; www.michel-bras.com

Head chef: *Michel and Sébastien Bras*

On the menu: *A range of dishes inspired by the Aubrac region*

Did you know? *Monday (when Bras is closed) is team-bonding day. This can involve staff in anything from grape picking to playing football*

Top tip: *Seasoned visitors recommend that you approach Bras from the south. That way your sense of what to expect can be heightened by crossing the dizzying cable-stayed road-bridge, Viaduc de Millau*

Approximate cost for two: *Bras has three set menus: 'Evasion et Terre' (€216 for two); 'Découverte et Nature' (€348 for two); and 'Légumes et Nature' (the vegetarian menu, €264 for two). Prices don't include wine. Rooms at the restaurant hotel start at €225 a night*

ARZAK

Juan Mari Arzak is one of the great characters of the culinary world. At 65, he may be the grand old man of Spain's new cuisine, but he has the energy and dynamism of a man one-third his age. His quest to reinvent Basque cuisine, inspired after attending a short course with French chef Paul Bocuse in 1976, has led him on a boundary-busting journey of discovery involving new techniques and unusual ingredients. Together with his talented daughter Elena, he continues that work today, in his 'flavour lab', or test kitchen, above his restaurant – attesting to his ambition to experiment and discover.

But despite the lab, with its library of 1,000 ingredients, and the stunning, modern presentation of the dishes, Arzak's cuisine is deeply rooted in tradition. This is hardly surprising when you consider the restaurant was previously owned by his parents, who themselves inherited it from his grandparents, who had opened a tavern on the site in 1897. Many of his creations are modern interpretations of classic Basque dishes, and local ingredients are key. It's just that sometimes, the local ingredients are a little unexpected: so a new dish for this year, hake with white clay, hints at Arzak's new interest in cooking with the earth.

Elena herself is a formidable cook, having trained at some of Europe's most prestigious restaurants including Le Gavroche and El Bulli. But as important as the food is, Arzak also stands out for its warmth and welcome, with Juan Mari's lust for life lighting up every corner of his establishment. The good news is that Juan Mari shows no sign of hanging up his whites. 'I won't leave the kitchen because otherwise my life makes no sense,' he says.

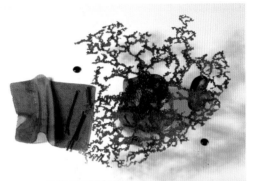

ON ORDER

273 Avenida Alcalde Elosegui, 20015 Donostia/ San Sebastián, Spain

+34 943 278 465; www.arzak.info

Head chef: *Juan Mari Arzak and Elena Arzak*

On the menu: *Hake and white clay; lobster with white olive oil*

Did you know? *Juan Mari has a passion for toys*

Top tip: *Don't book a table for November: Arzak is closed for holidays 2-26 November (and 15 June to 2 July), but open for the rest of the year*

Approximate cost for two: *€290, not including wine*

TETSUYA'S

A chef whose genial reputation precedes him, Tetsuya Wakuda sums up his *modus operandi* with humility: 'I made a lot of things up and, luckily, people like the way it tasted.' That, however, hardly begins to explain the rise of a visionary who can hold his own among the world's most outrageous culinary pace-setters.

Tetsuya left home, the Japanese industrial city of Hamamatsu, aged 22, arriving in Sydney with little English and a very limited grasp of what Australia was about. Nonetheless, he was soon working under Tony Bilson at Kinsela's, originally as a sushi chef, nourishing his love of food and learning fast.

Under Bilson, Wakuda learnt many of the classical French techniques that underpin his fusion cooking today. 'I started by doing some Japanese food – like sushi – and then Tony gave me the chance to do other things,' he says. 'He basically told me to trust my instincts and to try mixtures. He gave me the confidence and opportunity to test what I do.'

He left Kinsella's with one of the managers to set up Rose's nightclub, and within 18 months he had his own restaurant, Ultimo's. Six years later, in 1989, he opened the first tiny Tetsuya's with his wife, where

Chef's tasting menu

- Cold corn soup with saffron and vanilla ice-cream

- Smoked ocean trout and Avruga caviar

- Leek and crab custard

- Sashimi of big-eye tuna with wasabi and ginger vinaigrette

- Confit of Petuna Tasmanian ocean trout with konbu, daikon and fennel

- Seasonal green salad

- Ravioli of Queensland spanner crab with tomato and basil vinaigrette

- Grilled fillet of barramundi with braised baby fennel

- Twice-cooked deboned spatchcock with caper and olive jus

- Grilled wagyu beef with lime and wasabi

- Comte with lentils

- Apple sorbet with apple jelly

- Mont Blanc

- Caramelised fig with vanilla bean ice-cream

- Chocolate terrine with mascarpone and cognac Anglaise

'I made a lot of things up and, luckily, people like the way it tasted'

his unique fusion style – a distinctly Japanese emphasis on seasonality, zingy fresh ingredients, clean flavours and small, delicate plates, augmented by his newly acquired classical French techniques – began to draw crowds.

It wasn't, however, until 2000, when Tetsuya's moved to the Seagram's building in central Sydney that the wider world sat up and started to take notice. Tetsuya turned this impressive, modernist, heritage-listed building into a slick, contemporary restaurant in which diners eat looking out on to a serene Japanese bonsai garden. It's this combination, he maintains, that makes it 'his ideal restaurant'.

'But it's not just about the food being just right', he says. 'The aesthetics of the actual restaurant are also important to me. The dining experience should be one of visual as well as gastronomic pleasure.' He asked a friend, the late Akio Makigawa, to provide sculptures for the launch, while the ceramics on which many of his main dishes are presented are made exclusively by another friend Mitsuo Shoji.

There is no à la carte. For Tetsuya, the degustation menu is the very basis of his cooking. Diners are presented with 10 courses such as gazpacho with spiced tomato sorbet; West Australian marron with asparagus and truffle mayonnaise; and tartare of tuna with fresh wasabi to start. Tetsuya's signature dishes follow: confit of ocean trout served with unpasteurised ocean trout roe, followed by double-cooked deboned spatchcock with braised daikon and bread sauce, followed by a grilled fillet of grain-fed beef with sansho and shiitake mushrooms.

Courses are planned to build upon one another and careful consideration is given to each offering to ensure that it complements the last. It is dazzling, para-molecular stuff, created by a team of 21 chefs using all the latest gadgets and first-rate ingredients like sashimi-grade tuna, Tasmanian ocean trout and vegetables grown, often, to Tetsuya's specifications. (The restaurant houses an 'experimental kitchen', where new dishes are created and old ones reworked.)

It's this meticulous approach that has set Tetsuya Wakuda apart and helped build the restaurant up from the original Tetsuya's, a humble shopfront eatery where you could bring your own wine, to a culinary tour de force.

ON ORDER

529 Kent Street, Sydney, New South Wales 2000, Australia

+61 (0)2 9267 2900; www.tetsuyas.com

Head chef: *Tetsuya Wakuda*

On the menu: *Tian of caviar with soft smoked Petuna ocean trout, scallops mousse and quail egg bon bon*

Did you know? *Tetsuya's was voted Best Restaurant in Australasia in this year's awards*

Top tip: *It's notoriously hard to get a table here, so book in advance by phone or fax +61 (0)2 9262 7099*

Approximate cost for two: *Tetsuya's 12-course degustation menu is AUS$390 for two, and the accompanying wine course is AUS$180*

NOMA

For an area so rich in fresh ingredients, it has always been a bit of a disappointment to chef-owner René Redzepi that Nordic cuisine hasn't achieved the recognition it deserves. So, in 2003, he set about changing that by opening Noma, winning a Michelin star (the restaurant now has two) and placing Copenhagen and Nordic gourmet cuisine firmly on the culinary map.

It helps that Noma is located in one of the most picturesque parts of the city: Christianshavn, the man-made island brightly decorated with painted narrow houses and canal boats that always appear on the city's postcards. But although the scenery may entice you to Denmark's capital in the first place, it's Redzepi's unique showcasing of traditional Nordic cuisine that will make you return.

Not for him the olive oil, foie gras, sun-dried tomatoes or Mediterranean black olives that pepper some of the world's most sought-after tables. He fishes straight from his backyard: sourcing horse mussels, deep-sea crabs and langoustines from the Faeroe Islands; halibut, wild salmon, cod and seaweed and curds from Iceland; and lamb, musk ox, berries and the purest drinking water from Greenland. Not forgetting top-quality raw produce from Denmark itself.

The new Nordic kitchen

In November 2004, Claus Meyer and René Redzepi arranged a Nordic Cuisine Symposium attended by 12 of the region's top chefs – the result was the following 10-point manifesto:

- To express the purity, freshness, simplicity and ethics that we would like to associate with our region.

- To reflect the different seasons in the meals.

- To base cooking on raw materials whose characteristics are especially excellent in our climate, landscape and waters.

- To combine the demand for good taste with modern knowledge about health and wellbeing.

- To promote the Nordic products and the variety of Nordic producers – and to disseminate the knowledge of the cultures behind them.

- To promote the welfare of the animals and a sound production in the sea and in the cultivated as well as wild landscape.

- To develop new possible applications of traditional Nordic food products.

- To combine the best Nordic cooking procedures and culinary traditions with impulses from outside.

- To combine local self-sufficiency with a regional exchange of high-quality goods.

- To cooperate with representatives of consumers, other cooking craftsmen, agriculture, fishing industry, food industry, retail and wholesale industry, researchers, teachers, politicians and authorities on this joint project to the benefit and advantage of all in the Nordic countries.

'We wanted to combine advanced cooking techniques with the purity and simplicity of the Nordic region'

And nothing is pre-prepared or ordered in: 'We are smoking, salting, pickling, drying, grilling and baking our fish on slabs of basalt stone. We are also preparing our own vinegars and concocting our own distilled spirits,' he says. Which isn't to say that Noma doesn't make the most of the latest cutting-edge techniques – ones that Redzepi honed in his previous stints at the kitchens of The French Laundry in California, El Bulli in Spain and Jardin de Sens in France. 'We wanted to combine advanced cooking techniques with the purity and simplicity of the Nordic region. And to enhance the curative potential of the ingredients on which they are based.'

The restaurant occupies a 250-year-old shipping warehouse that has been leased to Redzepi and his business partner Claus Meyer by the local heritage trust. 'They wanted to create a restaurant that both reflected the warehouse's history and its new purpose history,' says Redzepi (the warehouse was originally used for the storage of sea salt and whale blubber). 'Claus and I went to the house. Then we brainstormed and talked about what we'd like to do and what would be possible.' The ambition was to create a new type of cuisine featuring ingredients sourced from the Nordic region. 'It should be subtle, light and involve things very close to their raw state, lightly cooked. It's a type of cooking that doesn't contain a lot of fat.'

The décor supports the approach: austere and yet warm, with dark wood furniture from Greenland, sheepskin throws, wooden floorboards and soft candlelight. The perfect setting in which to sample Noma's monthly changing menu of regional, seasonal dishes and classics, such as horseradish 'snow' with razor clams wrapped in parsley jelly with clam juice, dill and parsley – a remarkable, fresh-tasting dish combining in one mouthful, frozen 'snow' and fiery horseradish.

ON ORDER

Strandgade 93, 1401 Copenhagen K, Denmark

+45 3296 3297; www.noma.dk

Head chef-owner: *René Redzepi*

On the menu: *Look out for the Noma signature dish that uses 12 different kinds of onions and wild onion plants*

Did you know? *There are up to five foragers gathering wild foods for Noma*

Top tip: *On market day, Noma has a smaller lunch menu: three courses for DKK325*

Approximate cost for two: *The seven-course menu is DKK 1800 for two. Wine is DKK850 per person (one glass for each course)*

L'ASTRANCE

When you arrive at L'Astrance, the piece of paper that's put in your hands isn't so much a menu as a note to explain why there isn't one. What there is instead is a daily-changing multi-course tasting extravaganza that's dictated by what ingredients chef Pascal Barbot has been seduced by that morning, with some particular favourites almost always present. 'Our idea was to get together to create a new style of restaurant without a menu, just a surprise menu, which would be very serious but at the same time laid back,' says maitre d', Christophe Rohat. They opened in 2000, and it took them four years to get to the point at which they didn't have to have an à la carte offering, but now at lunch there's the choice of the three-course lunch menu, the five-course menu named after the season, or the eight-course Menu Saisonnier. The latter is the only choice at dinner, and it's the choice that the restaurant prefers because, says Rohat, 'that's how we best express ourselves.'

As well as offering diners a wonderful experience, there are obvious benefits to the restaurant when offering this kind of menu. 'It means the quality of our produce is irreproachable because everything we need for the day arrives that very morning,' says

Surprise surprise

The restaurant does have a wine list for those that want it, but all the menus can be served with surprise wines, collected by the sommelier. 'The idea is to really play with the idea of food and wine matching,' says Rohat. In fact the restaurant has garnered quite a reputation for this aspect of its activities, which is all the more remarkable considering that the menu changes daily, and the sommelier has no input or influence over what is served.

> **'Our idea was to get together to create a new style of restaurant without a menu, just a surprise menu, which would be very serious but at the same time laid back'**

Rohat. 'And, importantly for us, because of the surprise menu, there's no waste.'

And it's clearly a winning formula because the restaurant has been the hot ticket on the Paris scene since the 26-seater dining room opened. Diners have to wait, typically, a couple of months for a reservation.

Those lucky enough to score a table will find themselves in a room decorated in shades of slate, with bright yellow banquettes along the wall. A couple of tables are on a mezzanine level overlooking the restaurant, which is great for people watching, if the food doesn't prove sufficiently diverting (which is unlikely). The serving staff will first ascertain whether diners have any strong food dislikes or allergies, then ask, as the first courses are brought: 'Are you ready to be surprised?'

Barbot's influences are wide-ranging. He's well travelled and has brought back an understanding of Oriental ingredients, miso and lemongrass for instance, which he combines with classic luxury foods (langoustines, truffles etc) to great effect. The influence of his former mentor Alain Passard can be seen, too, in the absence of heavily reduced sauces or heavy butter and cream; this is very pure, elemental food in which the ingredients really shine through and suggest the very essence of themselves.

The sort of dishes that diners can expect include small shot glasses layered with vegetables, yoghurt and either milk or fruit foam. It might be cauliflower velouté, topped with a blend of yoghurt and saffron milk, or it could be cardamom yoghurt, carrot purée and mandarin foam, or peas, yoghurt and a lemon/mint foam according to season. This could be followed by a terrine of foie gras marinated in verjus

(the juice of under-ripe grapes) layered with thin slices of mushroom, dusted with porcini powder and served with a dollop of vivid yellow lemon purée. Some dishes are really surprising, such as fromage blanc with mashed potatoes and ice-cream, or soup infused with the flavour of toast.

ON ORDER

4 rue Beethoven, 75016 Paris, France

+33 (0)1 4050 8440

Head chef: *Pascal Barbot*

On the menu: *Celery velouté; black truffle coulis; Parmesan fondue and oyster cappuccino*

Did you know? *Astrance is a flower that grows in Barbot's native Auvergne*

Top tip: *It's hard to get a table here, as it seats just 26, but it's worth it. Book a month or two in advance*

Approximate cost for two: *€190 for the 'diner surprise' – €290 with wine pairings*

GAMBERO ROSSO

As known for his gruff and autocratic manner as he is for the edgy dishes he creates, Fulvio Pierangelini, chef-patron of Gambero Rosso (the 'red prawn') has been behind the stove of his restaurant five days a week since he opened it with his wife Emanuela (who tends front of house) in 1980. Not for him the vagaries of celebrity chefdom. A self-taught, intuitive chef, Pierangelini plays by his own rules; he chooses to ignore the food movements of his contemporaries and to eschew fashions and trends, leading his biographer, Raffaella Prandi, to nickname him 'il grande solista della cucina italiana', the great soloist of Italian cuisine. And yet, for the citizens of the Italian seaside town of San Vincenzo and all those who pass through it, the Gambero Rosso is the very pinnacle of modern Italian cuisine. Purely and simply, Pierangelini knows how to choose good products and he cooks them well.

Overlooking the cool blue Tyrrhenian Sea, it's little surprise that Pierangelini makes so much use of the local seafood in Gambero Rosso, but he also draws on inland Tuscan specialities (including pork produced on

his son's farm), all of which must first pass his personal quality check before being allowed on his menus.

Staples do exist, such as the celebrated chickpea purée with prawns. And it is these and his more recent classics that have led the Gambero Rosso to two Michelin stars and the title of best restaurant in Italy – *Le Figaro* restaurant critic François Simon went so far as calling it his favourite restaurant in the world.

At only 20 covers in the sea-view dining room, diners must book ahead. But it's worth the wait and journey, as Pierangelini and his wife greet diners personally, embellishing the meal with tips and anecdotes about its preparation and heritage.

ON ORDER

Piazza della Vittoria 13, 57027, San Vincenzo, Livorno, Italy

+39 (0)5 670 1021

Head chef: *Fulvio Pierangelini*

On the menu: *Burrata soup with ravioli of herring and roe*

Did you know? *Pierangelini recently won the title of Best Italian Chef in the Italian guidebook which shares its name with his restaurant, Gambero Rosso*

Top tip: *There are three menus to choose from, but the most popular by far is 'The Grand Menu of Fulvio Pierangelini', a menu totally at the discretion of the chef*

Approximate cost for two: *The set menus costs between €170 and €300 for two, not including wine*

RESTAURANT GORDON RAMSAY

Gordon Ramsay is a chef whose career has been built partly on the kind of technical excellence that inspires critics to describe it as 'cooking at the very highest level', 'startlingly delicious' and 'as good a meal as I've ever eaten in my life.' But partly also on his capacity to inspire others to excellence. Angela Hartnett, Stuart Gillies and Mark Sargeant are just some of his trusted lieutenants who uphold the name of the Ramsay empire even as they make their own names in the culinary world.

Ramsay does not come from a family of foodies. No glowing childhood memories of convivial times around the kitchen table for him. Or, as he puts it in his autobiography, *Humble Pie*, 'I did not pod beans at my grandmother's knee, gather forest mushrooms, or chase the farmyard hens.' In fact, it was only when his career as a footballer for Glasgow Rangers was

Clare Smyth

It's a good idea not to take Ramsay's outrageous pronouncements (such as 'Women can't cook to save their lives') at face value. Because the person responsible, along with executive chef Mark Askew, for upholding the reputation of this restaurant is a woman, head chef Clare Smyth. Her boss would be proud of her fierce determination and single-minded pursuit of perfection. She tastes everything that comes into the kitchen, and doesn't hesitate to send it back if quality is found to be lacking. She works from 7am until 1am, barely pausing to sit down, and rarely takes days off.

Clare learned about food from the local restaurant her mother managed near the Giant's Causeway in Northern Ireland, and about hard work and competitiveness from her father, a racehorse trainer. Smyth was 16 when she left home, against her parents' wishes, to take up a position as an apprentice at Grayshott Hotel in Surrey, which she combined with an NVQ at a college near Portsmouth. From there she went to the kitchens at Bibendum in London, and then to Cornwall to the St Enodoc Hotel for four years – with a six-month stint in Sydney sandwiched in between. Holidays were spent doing 'stages' in the kitchens of luminaries such as Michael Caines, Heston Blumenthal and the Roux brothers before starting at Restaurant Gordon Ramsay in 2002. She admits she had to work hard to be accepted in the male-dominated kitchen, and even harder when she took time out from Gordon Ramsay to train at the Louis XV in Monaco, for which she had to put herself through a four-week intensive French course. She now controls the kitchen in Chelsea in her signature style, with the minimum of fuss.

Smyth 's not the only woman to have benefited from Ramsay's tough brand of training. Before Smyth was Angela Hartnett, who joined Ramsay at Aubergine and now has a small group of restaurants under her own control, and both Simone Zanoni (who heads up the kitchen in Ramsay's Versailles operation) and Gemma Tuley (Foxtrot Oscar) are Restaurant Gordon Ramsay alumni.

'I did not pod beans at my grandmother's knee, gather forest mushrooms or chase the farmyard hens'

ended by injury that he went to catering college, at his mother's suggestion (his father thought that all cooking was a bit sissy). But he only really became properly inspired about food and restaurants – only tasted luxury ingredients such as foie gras and truffles for the first time – in the kitchens of Harvey's, in south London, run by the iron hand and ruled by the passions of fellow bad-boy Marco Pierre White. From there Ramsay worked with Albert Roux at Le Gavroche and eventually ended up in Paris working for Joël Robuchon and Guy Savoy.

He burst on to our screens in a fly-on-the-wall documentary that charted the opening of this first restaurant, with the financial backing of his father-in-law, Chris Hutcheson. The documentary forged the public's perception of Ramsay as foul-mouthed, tempestuous and passionate, and earned him – in spite of his 85 per cent staff retention rate since 1993 – a reputation as one of 'Britain's worst bosses', all impressions which to this day Ramsay has done nothing to dispel.

Fiercely competitive with his fellow high-profile foodies, he's not merely adversarial but vitriolic on occasion. AA Gill called him a 'wonderful chef, just a really second-rate human being'. So Ramsay threw him, and his dining companion Joan Collins out of his restaurant for being so mean (or for the publicity – one or the other). He's sounded off on subjects including women chefs, women drivers (earning him a reputation as a misogynist) and vegetarians.

It's redundant to say so, but the dining experience at Royal Hospital Road, the flagship restaurant of Gordon Ramsay Holdings, is in marked contrast to the fiery persona (the public one, at least) of its proprietor and founder. From the stylishly understated décor to the classically elegant French food, the experience represents sheer luxury.

ON ORDER

68 Royal Hospital Road, London SW3 4HP, UK

+44 (0)20 7352 4441; www.gordonramsay.com

Head chef: *Clare Smyth and executive chef Mark Askew*

On the menu: *Sautéed foie gras with roasted veal sweetbreads, Cabernet Sauvignon vinegar and almond; bitter chocolate cylinder with coffee granité and ginger mousse velouté*

Did you know? *The restaurant was redesigned in 2006 by David Collins Studio. The colour palette is warm white, and the space is multi-textured with mirrors, gold, glossy walls and leather dining chairs, lit by gorgeous chandeliers resembling molecules or solar systems*

Top tip: *If you want to get even closer to Ramsay's Michelin-starred cuisine, you can book a 'master class' at Restaurant Gordon Ramsay. These private lessons cost a whopping £6,000. See www.gordonramsay.com*

Approximate cost for two: *Three courses for £90 each, bottle of wine from £40*

L'ATELIER DE JOËL ROBUCHON

Legendary is an overused term, but it can be applied without hesitation to Joël Robuchon. Named Chef of the Century by the *Gault Millau* guide in 1989, Robuchon shocked the culinary world when he retired in 1996 at the age of just 50. He shocked the world again in 2003 when he burst back on to the Paris scene with his highly individual, upmarket take on a tapas bar.

The city queued around the smart 7th arrondissement for the opportunity to grab one of the 36 stools arranged around the open kitchen, to sample tasting plates of fresh mackerel on a thin tart with Parmesan shavings and olives; crispy langoustine fritter with basil pistou; and quail stuffed with foie gras. It was a formula for considerable success, and now an army of black-uniformed chefs work around the world in a series of Ateliers as far afield as Hong Kong and Las Vegas, all sporting variations on the original black, red and dark wood contemporary design.

Robuchon is a famously hard taskmaster, a relentless perfectionist. 'I was like a tortured child,'

Michelin man

Joël Robuchon restaurants have a total of 18 Michelin stars: His Atelier in Paris, number 14 on the 50 Best list, has two Michelin stars – those in London, New York, Tokyo and Las Vegas have one star each. The more formal restaurants in Monaco (Joël Robuchon Monte Carlo in the city's Hôtel Métropole), Paris (see picture above) and Tokyo at La Table de Joël Robuchon have two stars. But it's in Tokyo (at the Château Restaurant Joël Robuchon) and Las Vegas (at the Restaurant Joël Robuchon) where his most recent awards can be found. These both received three stars in 2007.

He's credited as the chef who led French cuisine away from the excesses – and excessive reductionism – of nouvelle cuisine

Gordon Ramsey said of his time in Robuchon's kitchen in his autobiography *Humble Pie*. 'You know how arrogant the French are. Extraordinary.' But it is that attention to detail that has led him to be credited as the chef who led French cuisine away from the excesses – and excessive reductionism – of nouvelle cuisine. It has also led him to 18 Michelin stars, the most held by any chef (his closest rival is Alain Ducasse with 15 and Ramsey with 12).

His head chef at the Parisian Atelier in his chain is Eric Lecerf, Robuchon's sous chef during his glory years at Jamin, from 1982 to 1989. Lecerf disappeared to the West Indies on Robuchon's retirement, before a stint at Le Chapon Fin, in the small southern city of Perpignan, where he was awarded a Michelin star.

When, in 1996, Robuchon took over the directorship of the newly created Restaurant de l'Astor in Paris, he lured his former protégé back to Paris to serve as his executive chef and he has remained at his side (and loyal in his absence) ever since. Robuchon may get the glory, but it is Lecerf who ensures that the food meets the quality that the public and his old master expects.

With a décor influenced by Japan, a tapas menu that is packed with French delicacies and prices that hardly reflect Robuchon's star status, it could be easy to be confused by the protocol. Fortunately, many of Robuchon's well-known creations can be found on the 'more substantial' menu that sits alongside the lighter tapas offerings. There's also a long chef's tasting menu, which features around 20 dishes in even small portions, from spiced crab to pig's trotters. And, if you're inspired by what you eat, you can even attempt to recreate it at home: Robuchon has recently launched his own French food magazine and an accompanying website, 'Cook like a chef' (*Cuisinez Comme un Chef*, www.cuisinezcommeunchef.fr), to show you how.

ON ORDER

5-7 rue de Montalembert, 75007 Paris, France

+33 (0)1 4222 5656; www.joël-robuchon.com

Head chef: *Philippe Braun and Eric Lecerf*

On the menu: *Pig's trotter on Parmesan toast*

Did you know? *The notoriously stern chef has a softer side: Eric Ripert of three-Michelin-starred Le Bernardin in New York says that Robuchon 'tugged at his hair and called him Coco' when he worked for him at Jamin*

Top tip: *Reservations are only accepted for the first sitting, so book early or chance your luck with the rest of Paris*

Approximate cost for two: *A choice of one main course and two tapas dishes costs €150 for two, including wine*

LE LOUIS XV

Le Louis XV is the flagship restaurant of über-restaurateur Alain Ducasse, whose culinary business interests are wide ranging and globe-spanning. In addition to high-profile restaurants in New York, Paris and London, as well as Tokyo and Las Vegas, there are auberges, the multi-ethnic, high-concept Spoon brand, bistros, a cooking school and a couple of Parisien baker/grocer-shop hybrids. The man has even developed dishes for the European Space Agency that could be made using food grown in space.

The menu speaks of its Mediterranean location, and is shot through with the gutsy, earthy flavours of the Provençal hinterland as well as the briny Mediterranean itself. It is divided into sections entitled 'The vegetable garden' (Provence garden vegetables with black truffle, olive oil, balsamic and salt), 'The sea' (locally-caught fish cooked with bouillabaisse stock), 'The woods, the fields' (seasonal dishes such as mushrooms or asparagus), 'The farm' (meat dishes) and 'Pastureland' (cheeses). But such apparent simplicity is very disingenuous, of course, because the skill with which these dishes are presented and served elevate them to a whole new level. And it's

Alain Ducasse – a career

Alain Ducasse was born in 1956 in the Landes region of south west France, into a family that reared ducks and geese for foie gras. Although he says his mother wasn't much of a cook, he describes being in his bedroom and smelling the delicious aromas wafting up from the kitchen where his grandmother was preparing meals as one of the formative experiences of his life. Indeed, it set him on the path to becoming a chef (though she didn't much like it when he told her the beans were overcooked).

In spite of parental misgivings (they wanted him to carry on with his academic studies) he was apprenticed to a local restaurant, but soon branched out to enjoy stints with some of the big names of 20th century French gastronomy: Michel Guérard, Roger Verge and Alain Chapel. Chapel in particular was an important influence, as it was he who was among the first to talk about the primacy of ingredients over technique. In 1984, he found his first independent success at the Hôtel Juana, Juan-les-Pins, but that same year he survived an air crash that killed all the other occupants of the small plane he was travelling in.

During his recovery (it was three years before he could walk unaided) he constructed menus in his head, drew on his sensory memory to concoct dishes, and became convinced that he didn't necessarily need a kitchen in order to be a chef. And so rather than retreat into himself after this appalling catastrophe, he chose to undertake more and more ambitious projects. In 1987 he was contracted by the Societé des Bains de Mer in Monaco to head up their Louis XV restaurant, on the understanding that the restaurant would have three Michelin stars within four years. The stars were his after the restaurant was a mere 33 months old. Alain Ducasse was exactly 33 years old at the time – the youngest chef to win the accolade.

'A restaurant is first and foremost a place to eat'

delivered in a setting that's so luxurious that anything else would be entirely incongruous. The restaurant could be a room from the Palace of Versailles, with ceiling frescos looking down on the luxuriously spaced tables (complete with small footstools on which the ladies can rest their designer bags). There are enormous flower arrangements, tiny silver birds by Christofle on every table, large wall mirrors, chandeliers and a view on to the bustle of the Place du Casino.

There was some scepticism when the robustly Mediterranean menu was launched (would Monaco's casino-going, moneyed elite go for something so rustic?), but Alain Ducasse's aim is to make haute cuisine as accessible as possible, because, as he says, 'A restaurant is first and foremost a place to eat'.

At the stoves on a daily basis is head chef Franck Cerutti, of whom Ducasse says: 'Franck Cerutti personifies the Mediterranean – it's in his blood and inspires all his work.' He grew up around Nice and wanted initially to be a farmer, but took up cooking instead, as this at least allowed him to stay in contact with his beloved local produce. He first worked with Ducasse at the Hotel Juana, and in spite of the fact that he'd already opened a place of his own, he returned to Le Louis XV when Ducasse needed a trusted hand in the kitchen when he was about to open in Paris.

In order to ensure that his various establishments throughout the globe embody the true Ducasse spirit, he seeks and nurtures chefs who are as likeminded as possible ('We're a little like a sect,' he confesses). Then Franck Cerutti trains them in the kitchens at Le Louis XV before sending them out into the world, testament to the fact that this restaurant is the true embodiment of the Ducasse sensibility. This, after all, is where it all began.

ON ORDER

Hôtel de Ville, Place du Casino, Monte Carlo 98 000, Monaco

+377 (0) 9806 8864; www.alain-ducasse.com

Head chef: *Franck Cerutti*

On the menu: *Gamberoni from San Remo served 'à la plancha' with marinated vegetables, lemon-thyme and clams*

Did you know? *Every diner uses over 50 pieces of tableware during their meal*

Top tip: *There are 18 types of bottled water available, 10 varieties of herbal tea on the fresh infusion trolley, and the sommelier Noël Bajor offers 950 different wines*

Approximate cost for two: *€380, not including wine*

ST JOHN

One feels one should be backing up to the entrance of St John in a van. It's so far removed from the flash, gaudy and ostentatious facades one associates with top restaurants that you could be forgiven for mistaking the entrance for the delivery bay. A paved entry leads to some utilitarian double doors, which open on to a light, bright, whitewashed room with a stone-flagged floor. Simple wooden tables and chairs lend it a faintly Shaker air, but in the end it looks pretty much like what it is: a barely converted smokehouse.

The restaurant was opened in October 1994 by seasoned restaurateur Trevor Gulliver and chef Fergus Henderson, who kept the somewhat austere feel of the original building in order to help customers address their own preconceptions about what dining in a nice restaurant should be about. 'The English are still having a slightly hard time going out to eat, they're not very good at it,' says Henderson. 'They seem to want marble and brass and paintings and long menus to act as crutches to tell them they're having a good time.' But Henderson has other ideas. He wants the diners themselves, happily enjoying their meals, to be the decoration. 'You sometimes see tables of people hovering, not quite sure why they've been told to come

Birth of a classic:
How bone marrow with parsley salad came to be

'The bone marrow is an almost cheekily simple dish. How it came about was, a week or so before we opened, I went to see *La Grande Bouffe*, and there's a scene where they're all tucking into big bones, and I thought: "There's a dish for me". The parsley salad came about when I was working in this dodgy club in Notting Hill and Rowley (Leigh, formerly of Kensington Place) came in after work and asked for a salad, and all I had left was parsley, so I made a parsley salad. So I had those two things lurking in my head and they seemed perfectly happy to go together.'

'There's really no reason why something that tasted good a hundred years ago shouldn't taste good today'

to this rather dour, white restaurant, but then they sit down and order and have some wine and start having a really good time, and that's such a lovely feeling.'

Henderson is highly regarded in the restaurant community for (re)introducing Britain to its culinary heritage, and for being unafraid to offer menu items that might initially be offputting to the less seasoned diner (chitterlings, bone marrow, ox heart). But these dishes aren't on the menu to invite acts of bravado, they're there because they taste good, and because it simply makes sense to use as much of the animal as possible. And on any given day there will also be dishes that feature whatever fresh fish has just been landed, top-notch British cheeses and dishes such as potted beef and pigeon pie that sound as if they're from the menu of an Edwardian shooting party.

But Henderson's food is not intended as a manifesto, and it's certainly not about harking back to 'the good old days'. 'My food isn't intended as any kind of jingoistic statement, and nor is it a kind of rose-tinted, sticky-toffee-pudding view of the world – I hate sticky toffee pudding, though I love a good syrup sponge. It's just that there's really no reason why something that tasted good a hundred years ago shouldn't taste good today'

This all seems so logical, yet when St John burst on to the scene to universal acclaim in the mid 1990s, Henderson really seemed to be doing something new. Not that he's ever considered himself a trailblazer: 'I don't think there was anything particularly pioneering about what we did, it just struck me as very odd that most countries have restaurants that reflect their own cultures and we don't, other than rather strange, olde-worlde restaurants, so I thought we should try and create something that was reflective of its own culture. It wasn't pioneering, it was just common sense.'

ON ORDER

26 St John Street, London EC1M 4AY, UK

+44 (0)20 7251 0848; www.stjohnrestaurant.com

Head chef: *Chris Gillard and Fergus Henderson*

On the menu: *Roast bone marrow and parsley salad*

Did you know? *Fergus Henderson is a staunch believer in the enlivening power of a slice of seed cake and a glass of Madeira taken for elevenses*

Top tip: *The restaurant has a small private dining room, which holds a maximum of 18 people, where you can feast on roast suckling pig, by prior arrangement*

Approximate cost for two: *£100 (including wine)*

JEAN GEORGES

Jean-Georges Vongerichten calls his eponymous restaurant in New York 'the expression of [his] 34 years as a chef', considering it to be the ultimate product of his decades of classical French training and, he says, the magic and energy of New York City itself. He loves it here and diners can tell: Jean Georges was awarded its third Michelin star in 2004 and has retained it for the past four years.

The restaurant's setting couldn't be more impressive or grandiose: it is the showcase restaurant of the Trump International Hotel and Tower and the décor (and views) are exactly what you might expect from such an illustrious setting – from the hand-laid mosaic floor and shimmering marble surfaces to the white Bernardaud china and the custom-made Sheffield cutlery. And the service is just as heady as the venue, with the dishes cooked in front of diners in an open kitchen, before the final touches are performed at the side of guests' tables, where lobsters are cracked, meat is sliced and desserts are scooped with an almost self-conscious flourish.

But, ultimately, as Vongerichten is the first to point out, Jean Georges is about much more than its setting.

Chef's tasting menu

Chef Vongerichten assortment of signature dishes ($148)

- *Egg caviar*
- *Bay scallops, caramelised cauliflower and caper-raisin emulsion*
- *Young garlic soup with thyme and sautéed frog legs*
- *Turbot with Château-Chalon sauce*
- *Lobster tartine, lemongrass and fenugreek broth with pea shoots*
- *Broiled squab, onion compote and corn parncake with foie gras*
- *A choice of desserts, including pomegranate sorbet with fresh
  pomegranate seeds and chocolate poppy seed cake, Meyer lemon
  curd, Halva powder*

'I try to create places that fulfill people's cravings'

'My restaurant philosophy is all about creating cravings. I try to create places that fulfill people's cravings. People become comfortable with a couple of items on the menu in a particular restaurant and I keep those favourites on the menu all the time. People come back for the food that they are comfortable with and then again maybe about 30 per cent of the people, especially in New York City, want new items on the menu when they revisit my restaurants.'

This is elegant fine dining at its very best, with clean, intense and often simple flavours, which at times bely the theatre of its service and the colourful nature of its presentation. Clearly influenced by time spent in Asia, Vongerichten's cuisine is nonetheless never too far from its French roots. The result is an exciting combination that draws on wild edible plants and oils infused with herbs and spices, resulting in dishes like halibut steamed with honshimeji mushrooms and lemongrass consommé; smoked squab a l'orange; and heirloom watermelon gazpacho.

Born and raised on the outskirts of Strasbourg in Alsace-Lorraine, Jean-Georges' earliest family memories are about food. 'I would wake every morning to the most wonderful smells,' he says, 'and I quickly became known as "the palate" to my family, tasting each sauce and dish, recommending salt or some more herbs.' His career was decided on a visit to the Michelin-starred Auberge de l'Ill, where he later became apprentice to chef Paul Haeberlin. From there he went to work with Paul Bocuse and Louis Outhier before moving to the US and making his name at the Lafayette restaurant in Boston.

He opened his first restaurant, Jo Jo, in 1991; followed four years later by his next venture, the Orient-inspired Vong, of which there are now three more dotted in London, Hong Kong and Chicago. Jean Georges may be his most successful venture to date, but it hasn't stopped there; he opened The Mercer Kitchen at the stylish Mercer Hotel in SoHo in 1998.

ON ORDER

1 Central Park West, New York, NY 10023, USA

+1 212 299 3900; www.jean-georges.com

Head chef: *Mark Lapico*

On the menu: *Lobster tartine, lemongrass and fenugreek broth with pea shoots*

Did you know? *Chef Jean-George Vongerichten has his own blog (www.jeangeorge.blogspot.com) on which he offers advice and recipes, as well as his musings about international cuisine*

Top tip: *If your wallet won't extend to the tasting menus (see below), you can also select a choice of three dishes for $98 per person*

Approximate cost for two: *Both the 'Chef Vongerichten assortment of signature dishes' and the seasonal menu (seven courses) cost $296 for two, not including service or wine*

ALAIN DUCASSE PLAZA ATHÉNÉE

In 2000 the Hotel Plaza Athénée had just been given a multi-million pound makeover, and was busy basking in its position amid the top-end designer boutiques and temples to couture on the Avenue de Montaigne.

The hotel needed a chef with a reputation for surefootedness, with high-end ingredients and the ability to hire and inspire the best teams in the business. They needed Alain Ducasse. He already had a restaurant in Paris as part of his starry portfolio, but decided that to move it from the location he'd inherited from Joël Robuchon on the Avenue Raymond Poincaré would be mutually beneficial. So move it he did, and there it remains, rubbing shoulders with the movie stars and fashion moguls who hang out in the swanky 8th arrondissement.

Though both the Louis XV and the Plaza Athénée restaurants exude luxury, and represent wonderful gastronomic experiences, the latter is certainly not an 'outpost' of the former. Ducasse insists it's not about building an empire of identikit luxury restaurants, but

A touch of class

As befits its location, 'elegant' is the restaurant's faintly intimidating dress code, and you'd better take heed; it wouldn't do to be too outshone by the waiting staff. Their uniforms were designed by Monaco couturier Georges Feghaly (famous for his limited-edition silk ties, of which Ducasse has a collection). Their black jackets, grey trousers, white shirts and grey twill ties are described on the restaurant's website as: 'A perfect blend of elegance and good quality'. To add to all the glamour, the restaurant's interior was re-imagined in 2005 by top international designer Patrick Jouin. Mirrors, gilding, candelabras and floor-to-ceiling windows and doors remind you that you're in one of the fanciest hotels, in one of the fanciest streets, in arguably the fanciest city in the world. But at the same time, touches such as a deconstructed 'chandelier' made from thousands of individually hung Swarovski crystals and a clock that ticks, but does not tell the time, play on twin themes of 'magic' and 'poetry'. Jouin has his feet on the ground, though; he was also responsible for designing the 'Vélib' bicycle rental stations now so ubiquitous in Paris.

'Turbot without genius is better than genius without turbot'

rather creating something appropriate to the city, the environment in which he finds himself. 'My passion is to know whether I can make a restaurant in London, Tokyo or New York that's right for them,' he says. 'But always with a difference. I don't want to do the same thing over again.' So there are no signature dishes that cross over into different restaurants, no corporate logos that unite them – fonts and furnishings are the kind of detail over which Ducasse likes to obsess personally, according to the personality of each restaurant.

The menu at the Plaza Athénée has been tuned to the palates of the ultra-rich Avenue Montaigne set; their comforting roast chicken dinner comes in the form of roast Bresse chicken with spring vegetables and morille mushrooms à peine crèmes (barely creamed), instead of blinis, their Iranian osetra caviar comes with langoustines and fragrant broth. Lots of exalted ingredients then, but for Ducasse cooking is 60 per cent ingredients, 40 per cent technique, not just the expression of a chef's skill superimposed on a product. As he puts it: 'Turbot without genius is better than genius without turbot.'

When Ducasse first opened his restaurant in Paris, the Michelin guide took away one of his stars at the restaurant in Monaco, as if to rebuke him for having the temerity to run kitchens at that level in multiple locations. The stars were restored however, and the trend for charismatic chefs to run restaurants in several locations has continued unabated. When asked who does the cooking when he's not in the kitchen, Ducasse is not the only chef credited with replying, 'The same person who does it when I am there'. Because for him it's about sharing his knowledge, understanding and expertise: 'There are no secrets in the kitchen,' he says. 'I share everything I know. There's a lot of hard work, but no secrets.'

In common with many of this trusted lieutenants, the head chef at Alain Ducasse Plaza Athénée was trained in the kitchens of the Louis XV in Monaco. Christophe Moret studied at hotel school in Blois in 1986, then worked with Bruno Cirino and Jacques Maximin before joining Alain Ducasse in Monaco in 1990. He then became became sous chef at Restaurant Alain Ducasse in Paris, Avenue Raimond Poincaré, then chef at Spoon Food & Wine in Paris. 'Alain Ducasse lays out the broad strokes,' he says. 'It's up to me to fill in the lines.'

ON ORDER

25 Avenue de Montaigne, 75008 Paris, France

+33 (0)1 5367 6500; www.alain-ducasse.com

Head chef: *Alain Ducasse and Christophe Moret*

On the menu: *Turbot with shellfish bouquet and parsley juice; or roe deer with winter vegetables and poivrade reduction*

Did you know? *The waiting staff's outfits were designed by couturier George Feghaly, based on their own definition of 'the ideal uniform'*

Top tip: *Closed Saturdays, Sundays and public holidays. Annual closure mid July to mid August, and mid December to 31 December*

Approximate cost for two: *€290 including service, but not wine*

HAKKASAN

Ever since it opened in 2001, Hakkasan has managed the near impossible feat of being both the 'it' destination for the see-and-be-seen fashion crowd (do they actually eat anyway?) and the serious foodie (who will want to try everything on the menu).

Most people, on arriving at Hakkasan for the first time, worry that they've gone to the wrong place – it used to be an underground car park and from the outside it shows – but what better way to make sure that the interior (which, admittedly, would be stunning in any location) surprises and delights with its glamour? It's cavernous, seating 130 in the main dining area, which is arrived at via a sinuous staircase, and it really feels as if one is entering another world. Moodily lit and minimalist, with distinctive Oriental accents (such as the intricately carved wooden screens used as room dividers), there's an edge of decadence and excitement.

Regulars rave at the quality of the fresh, impeccably prepared dim sum (they make everything to order here rather than circulating a trolley) such as the emerald green dumplings stuffed with prawn and chive, or the venison char siu puffs. Hardcore foodies sometimes cavil at the lack of extremities, innards and obscurities on the menu (there's no them-and-

The chef behind the celebrity

The importance of Alan Yau as a figurehead behind Hakkasan harks back to an earlier era than today's celebrity-chef dominated restaurant world. The person in charge of turning out such visually stunning and palate-pleasing dishes as the famous jasmine tea smoked chicken at Hakkasan is Tong Chee Hwee. Born in 1963, he started his career, aged 18, at the Happy Valley Chinese restaurant in Singapore before moving to their Kuala Lumpur restaurant. He then moved back to Singapore to work, and it was here that he was discovered by Alan Yau, overseeing the kitchens at the highly regarded Chinese restaurant at the Ritz Carlton. Yau was on the lookout for a top chef, and persuaded him to move to London in 2001, along with a couple of key kitchen personnel. The presence of Tong Chee Hwee gave Yau's project a foundation on which to build a following of food enthusiasts, many of whom were ready to dismiss the restaurant as just another fly-by-night fashionista haunt. But his skill in presenting the complex flavours of Chinese dishes with freshness and vitality brings a modern flair that's in keeping with the Hakkasan ethos, and Yau's vision.

Ever since it opened in 2001, Hakkasan has managed the near impossible feat of being both the 'it' destination for the see-and-be-seen fashion crowd and the serious foodie

us menu separatism here). And Alan Yau himself acknowledges that the menu would be different if the restaurant were in Hong Kong, because people there have a different palate – he feels Londoners crave strong tastes, and the waiting list seems to bear out his hypothesis.

Yau – who is also the entrepreneurial genius behind noodle chain Wagamama – has a gift for developing a concept and getting the details right. From the menu down to the soundtrack, diners get the sense of being somewhere edgy, connected, on-trend. Born in Hong Kong, he was raised by his grandparents there until he was 11, when his parents (who had moved to King's Lynn to set up a Chinese takeaway) sent for him and his siblings. He worked in the family business before leaving to go to college, and then afterwards his father helped him to establish his own takeaway business in Peterborough, which soon recouped the initial investment. A stint of franchisee training with McDonald's back in Hong Kong, followed by work with KFC in London was enough to start Yau along his chosen path of refining restaurant concepts, first with Wagamama, then with Busaba Eathai.

Hakkasan was restaurateur Alan Yau's 'bit of fun' after he sold his fledgling Wagamama chain (there were only two at the time; it's now a global brand). It was quite a change in focus; glamorous, high-end Hakkasan is a world away from the egalitarian ethos of the communal tables that Wagamama represents. He recently sold Hakkasan and its sibling all-day dim sum joint, Yauatcha, to Tasameem, a division of the Abu Dhabi Investment Authority for over £30m, but this time has retained control, and will be extending the brand to branches worldwide in the near future.

ON ORDER

8 Hanway Place, London W1T 1HD, UK

+44 (0)20 7927 7000; www.hakkasan.com

Head chef: *Tong Chee Hwee*

On the menu: *Silver cod in Chinese honey and champagne, Peking duck with royal Beluga caviar, grilled wagyu beef with enoki mushrooms and soya*

Did you know? *Hakkasan takes its name from Hakka, a Chinese nomadic ethnic group, and 'san' is a respectful Japanese suffix approximating to 'Mr' or 'Mrs'*

Top tip: *If you can't book into Hakkasan, try Alan Yau's all-day dim sum restaurant, Yauatcha, in Soho*

Approximate cost for two: *Menu prices range from £5.50 to £280 (for the braised supreme dried whole Japanese abalone) for individual menu items. Wine from £25 to £1,722*

LE BERNARDIN

Siblings Maguy and Gilbert Le Coze were just teenagers when they started working in the restaurant of their parents' inn, the Hotel de Rhuys, at Port Navalo, a fishing village in Brittany. With Maguy in the dining room and Gilbert in the kitchen, honing the skills taught by his father and grandfather, the two made an impressive pair. So much so that their family provided the backing to enable them to run a summer disco for tourists. After the season ended, they took their skills to the Alps and developed the technical and business skills to consider opening an establishment on a grander scale. This they did when in 1972 they opened a small restaurant in Paris called Le Bernardin, named after a food-and-wine-loving order of monks. True to the pair's roots, the restaurant was dedicated to fish and seafood, and in spite of its narrow specialism it gained the kind of widespread acclaim that in 1981 necessitated a move to bigger premises. Encouraged by their American clientele and by their success in Paris, the Le Cozes decided to open in New York City in 1986.

Eric Ripert – a career

Born in Antibes, France, in 1965 Eric Ripert had begun his love affair with food as an eater. 'I've been interested in cooking all my life,' he says. 'Not to work but to eat. I was always a gourmand. I thought if I was in the kitchen I'd be able to eat all the time. I was a real cookie monster.'

His family provided the inspiration he needed: 'My mother was an excellent cook, I was very influenced by her refinement. She loved presentation, she has a good instinct and her food always tasted really good.'

The family had moved from Antibes to Andorra when Ripert was a boy, so when at 15 he was encouraged to switch to vocational training, it was a toss-up between culinary school and training to become a mountain guide, as he also loved the outdoor life amid Andorra's rugged scenery. With the support of his parents he opted to train as a chef in Perpignan. When his training ended at 17, he moved to Paris. 'I wrote to all the three-star restaurants in France, and Le Tour d'Argent answered.' After two years there he went to Jamin to work with Jöel Robuchon, where after several years (and completion of his military service) he ended up as chef poissonnier – in charge of cooking the fish.

In 1989 Ripert was sent by Robuchon to the United States to work as sous chef to Jean-Louis Palladin at the Watergate Hotel in Washington DC. His contract was up after 18 months and he decided to move to New York City, where he worked with David Bouley until offered the job at Le Bernardin with Maguy and Gilbert Le Coze.

'From Robuchon I learned technique, but Jean-Louis kind of opened my mind and freed it from all the technique. He was an artist and he helped me understand what creativity was. But Gilbert really taught me how to be a chef. A cook is your core and a chef is your title. When you're a good chef you know how to manage your restaurant, your technique and your team – Gilbert taught me that,' he says.

'When you're a good chef you know how to manage your restaurant, your technique and your team – Gilbert taught me that'

After selling the Parisian restaurant to build on their success in America, the Le Cozes opened Brasserie Le Coze in Coconut Grove, Florida, and in 1994, they opened a second Brasserie Le Coze, in Atlanta, Georgia. By this time, Gilbert had been joined in the kitchen in New York by Eric Ripert, and so when in 1994 Gilbert died suddenly of a heart attack, Ripert took over the kitchens. His technique, artistry and managerial capability (see opposite page) ensured that Ripert did not allow standards to slip, and Le Bernardin remains one of the key destination dining spots in New York City.

The room itself is often described, rather unflatteringly, as corporate and unromantic, but what elevates the restaurant beyond mere concerns about décor is the sheer quality of the fish (it has been said that before Le Bernardin, only Japanese restaurants dared to serve fish raw) and the way the kitchen prepares it. Ripert understands both the important of freshness and how to tailor his preparation to the variety. 'I love cooking fish,' he says. 'It's very delicate. Technically you have to be extremely precise, and the way you tune a sauce for fish is more difficult than for meat. You have to be much more sensitive.' Ripert's take on surf and turf – with tuan and Kobe beef 'Korean BBQ' style and fresh kimchi, or his baked lobster with candied ginger, port and tamarind showcase his bold style.

Ripert continues to evolve his menu while remaining committed to the classical tradition. He's influenced a great deal by his travels, though says that it often takes a while for different influences to soak themselves into his cuisine. 'Creativity is not like pushing a button, it comes sporadically and in waves. I try not to force my mind to create. I go somewhere, I absorb, I store up feelings and ideas about food, and it comes back later on and bombards me.'

ON ORDER

155 West 51st Street, Midtown, New York, NY 10019, USA

+1 212 554 1515; www.le-bernardin.com

Head chef: *Eric Ripert*

On the menu: *Masala-spiced crispy black bass, and Peking duck with green papaya salad in a rich ginger-cardamom broth*

Did you know? *Growing up in Andorra, Ripert hoped to be a mountaineer*

Top tip: *For special occasions, you can book Les Salons Bernardin, the private dining room where Uma Thurman held her baby shower. Quietly secluded, it can accommodate up to 90 guests, but there's also a more intimate room for up to 16 guests*

Approximate cost for two: *The fixed-price lunch menu is $128, the fixed-price dinner menu is $214 and the tasting menu is $360 for two*

ALINEA

When chef Grant Achatz opened Alinea in Chicago in May 2005, it was hotly anticipated, to say the least. Achatz had been talking about his plans to an online community of top-end restaurant goers since he closed his restaurant, Trio, in nearby Evanston the previous July, and the buzz surrounding the opening of Alinea was pretty deafening.

Achatz comes from a family of restaurateurs; his parents and grandparents ran modest, diner-style operations where the food was prepared from scratch, and very good, but of modest ambition. This was enough to inspire Achatz to be a chef. He went to culinary school straight from high school and from there worked his way up the culinary ladder before alighting at The French Laundry in California where he worked under chef Thomas Keller for four years. He realised, though, that he was interested in developing a cooking style of his own. 'My dream was to build a 'container' that mimicked, supported or exemplified the food,' he said. This eventually led to his partnership with Nick Kokonas and the launch of Alinea.

What they have created is a setting that does not recede into the background, but forms part of the restaurant experience. There's a strong element of

Martin Kastner

As Achatz's style started to evolve, he began to feel that there was a mismatch between the food that had emerged from all the new techniques that were out there and the serving vessels and utensils being used to eat them: 'We were serving this hyper-modern food on plates and bowls, and eating them with forks and knives and spoons that were virtually unchanged in 300 years,' he says. For him it didn't make sense either aesthetically or functionally. 'Some of these new techniques enable you to create interesting textures and very delicate things, it's just so inappropriate to put them on a plate.' So he began to search for somebody who'd be interested in developing the service pieces that would be appropriate for this style of food, and he found Czech artist and designer Martin Kastner. He had set up a design agency, Crucial Detail, in 1998, and was himself interested in the challenge of trying to reformulate how people eat and experience food. His first assignment was to devise a 'delivery system' for frozen hibiscus tea (he came up with a lollipop-like tripod) and since then he has gone on to produce more than 50 pieces for the restaurant, such as 'the squid', which is like an upturned whisk, to hold small dainty items, and the 'bow', on to which food – such as their butterscotch bacon – can be clipped as if on a washing line. These items help define the identity of the restaurant almost as much as the food. 'Sometimes I'll come up with a food concept that requires a special service piece, or he might come up with an idea and I'll come up with the food to go with it. It's a great collaboration, and a lot of fun,' says Achatz.

'You shouldn't feel you can't laugh out loud. You're here to have fun'

playfulness; the blank hallway one first enters appears to narrow uncomfortably, but a door activated by a motion sensor suddenly opens to admit diners to the restaurant proper, where they are greeted. So from the very first, expectations are subverted. Much, though, is traditional; if the room itself is minimalist, it's also extremely comfortable, modern and relaxed. 'You shouldn't feel you can't laugh out loud,' says Achatz. 'You're here to have fun.'

What you will experience, whether you choose the eight-, 12- or 24-course menu, is a cavalcade of small courses, presented in ways calculated to surprise and delight. Says Achatz: 'There are lots of things that you'll recognise, but a lot that you won't, because they're pushed in different directions texturally or aesthetically.' For example the peanut butter and jelly 'sandwich' is a peeled grape dipped in peanut butter cream and wrapped in a paper-thin layer of brioche. Or there's 'hot potato/cold potato' – essentially a chilled potato soup in a paraffin wax bowl with a cube of Parmesan, cube of chilled butter, a piece of chive, a hot potato and a slice of truffle suspended over it on a pin. The diner is instructed to pull out the pin to bring the ingredients together and enjoy the interplay of temperature, texture and flavour. Aromas are also brought into play to enhance the experience. For example, dishes might be placed on pillows that slowly deflate to release aromas that have been pumped inside.

The Alinea team refer to their kind of cuisine as 'progressive American', rejecting in particular the molecular gastronomy label with which some people are determined to pin them down. Achatz maintains he is trying to create the opposite of a sterile, scientific experience. 'We want it to be like experiencing performance art,' he says. And he adds that diners can expect to have a radically different experience every time they dine at the restaurant.

ON ORDER

1723 N Halsted Street, Chicago, Illinois 60614, USA

+1 312 867 0110; www.alinearestaurant.com

Head chef-owner: *Grant Achatz*

On the menu: *'The whole identity of the restaurant is constant evolution. We don't want to have signature dishes, we want to continually create'*

Did you know? *The Alinea book's broken a cardinal rule of American cookbooks: all measurements are metric*

Top tip: *There's no signage outside to tell you you're in the right place, just a valet parking sign. So check the address twice*

Approximate cost for two: *12-course tasting menu $145, 20+ course 'tour' menu $225, add another 70 per cent to this if you want to try the wine pairings*

LE GAVROCHE

When brothers Albert and Michel Roux opened Le Gavroche in 1967, London had no restaurant culture to speak of – the wealthy ate in private clubs or hotel dining rooms, the less well off had to make do with Lyons Corner Houses or cheap and cheerful trattoria.

The sons and grandsons of charcutiers, both were trained as patissiers and had worked as chefs in private homes before coming to London. At that time for bureaucratic reasons it was cheaper and easier to establish a restaurant in London than Paris. So – with the financial help of their aristocratic former employers – the brothers opened their restaurant on Lower Sloane Street and the 50-seater restaurant was soon full every night, with Michel in the kitchen one week, while Albert took the orders, and roles reversed the next.

At first, obtaining top-class ingredients such as foie gras and the best poulets de Bresse was a problem. Because Britain didn't join the Common Market until 1973, there were stringent customs controls on the import of fresh and raw foods. The entry of Britain into Europe came not a moment too soon for the Roux, as they had just opened The Waterside Inn in Bray, Berkshire, and needed luxury ingredients.

Service
Silvano style

A native of Padua, Italy, Silvano Giraldin went to catering college and worked in Italy, Belgium and France before arriving as a junior waiter at Le Gavroche in 1971. He was promoted to general manager in 1975, and since then has been responsible for the training and development of a whole generation of service staff. Much in the same way as the kitchens of the restaurant have spread their influence far and wide, Giraldin can claim responsibility for training such service personnel as Michel Lang of the Louis XV in Monte Carlo and Jean-Claude Breton of Restaurant Gordon Ramsay.

For Giraldin, there's no great secret to good service. 'Anybody can do it if they have the right attitude,' he says. 'Good service is a job. If you're paid to do it, do it with a smile and do it well. It's not the same as servility. If you feel servile you're not doing it right.'

'Good service is a job. If you're paid to do it, do it with a smile and do it well'

Service at Le Gavroche is much more theatrical than elsewhere, with more table-side carving, synchronised cloche-lifting and trolley wielding than in many other restaurants. 'Maybe some people will call us pompous,' says Giraldin. 'After all, the food tastes the same whether it comes with a cloche or not. But it's a style that we want to preserve. We think it's great fun, and people love the fact that they get a totally different experience at Le Gavroche.'

Giraldin has some advice for diners, too: 'We love it when customers ask questions,' he says. 'But, please, ask the right person! Don't ask the person pouring the water how the Château Lafite is drinking, that's what the sommelier is there for.'

In 1981 the pair moved from Lower Sloane Street to their present site on Upper Brook Street in Mayfair, but this placed the relationship between the brothers under strain, and resulted in Albert taking sole control of Le Gavroche, while Michel moved out to The Waterside Inn. Michel Roux Jr, Albert's son, took control of the kitchen in 1991 when his father retired at the age of 55. Before taking over, Michel had been working at the family's other establishments across London, having trained in France and Hong Kong under such legends as Alain Chapel.

Le Gavroche's cuisine had always been typically French, and a change of chef did nothing to alter that. Michel Roux Jr's contribution, however, has been to lighten up the menu and reduce the restaurant's reliance on creamy sauces and rich, buttery dishes (that said, the soufflé Suissesse, a Gruyere soufflé given a second baking on double cream is a classic that remains on the menu to this day). 'One of the secrets of our success is that we've stayed true to our roots,' says Michel. 'We're a classical French restaurant. But classical doesn't necessarily mean heavy or rich. Indulgent, yes, but it's also about showing off the best ingredients and not masking the food in any way.'

'Clubby' is the adjective perhaps most often employed to describe the décor at Le Gavroche. At street level there's a bar where diners can enjoy a pre-dinner drink before descending to basement level where dark green walls and a low ceiling create a hushed atmosphere that's in contrast to the clamour of some of London's other top restaurants. There's something charmingly old-fashioned about the service; sparkling silver cloches are simultaneously removed with a flourish (without irony) and one diner (usually the woman) in a party of two will get a menu *sans prices* (lest she suffer an attack of the vapours, presumably – dining here is certainly not cheap).

ON ORDER

43 Upper Brook Street, London W1K 7QR, UK

+44 (0)20 7408 0881; www.le-gavroche.co.uk

Head chef: *Michel Roux Jr*

On the menu: *Soufflé Suissesse*

Did you know? *Famous alumni of the kitchens at Le Gavroche include Marco Pierre White, Gordon Ramsay, Pierre Koffman of La Tante Claire, Marcus Wareing of Petrus, Philip Howard of The Square, Martin Wishart of Restaurant Martin Wishart and many others*

Top tip: *The £48 set-price lunch at Le Gavroche includes canapés, three courses with wine and water, coffee and petits fours, making it one of the best-value lunches in town*

Approximate cost for two: *Set dinner tasting menu £95 each (£150 including wine)*

DAL PESCATORE

To get to Dal Pescatore, intrepid diners need to be prepared. Prepared to negotiate a winding road, squint at maps in the dark, possibly ask for directions in halting Italian, probably have a falling-out with their driving companion/map reader, ask themselves if they should have taken that turning, and then, as they feel the gravitational pull of its relaxing ambience… breathe.

The restaurant is located in the middle of the Parco dell'Oglio Sud, near a tiny hamlet called Runate whose inhabitants number only in the double digits. But it's not right to say it's off the beaten path. In fact epicures, gourmets and pleasure seekers have been beating a path to this restaurant's door for decades, comfortable in the knowledge that they'll get peerless food and a genuinely warm welcome.

It started out modestly in the fisherman's hut at the side of a small lake, to which the fisherman-owner Antonio would bring his catch for his wife Teresa to cook and serve to whichever guests happened by on their bicycles. They called the restaurant – more of a tavern, really – Vini e Pesce, wine and fish.

From the kitchen
Tortelli di zucca (serves 4)

Ingredients

150g yellow pumpkin, roasted

20g Amaretto biscuits, finely ground

50g mostarda di frutta senapata (fruit pickled in mustard; use a teaspoon of dried mustard as an alternative)

20g Parmigiano-Reggiano cheese, grated

Pepper, salt, nutmeg, cloves and cinnamon

For the pasta

1 full egg + 1 egg yolk (60g + 30g)

100g white pasta flour '00'

A pinch of salt

For the sauce

50g butter

20g Parmigiano-Reggiano cheese, grated

Method

Push the roasted pumpkin through a sieve to make a purée. Add to this the ground amaretto biscuits, the mustard, the grated cheese and all the accompanying spices. Let the mix rest in the refrigerator while you prepare the pasta. For the pasta, add the egg to the pile of flour and mix and knead until it is of an adequate consistency to pass through the pasta machine. Once you have passed it through the pasta machine on its thinnest setting, cut squares of 8cm by 8cm to use for the tortelli. In each of these squares of pasta, add a spoonful (around 6-8g) of the pumpkin mixture. Fold the squares diagonally in half to hold the mixture and press firmly to seal the edges. Cook the finished pasta in boiling water for around five minutes before serving with melted butter and grated Parmigiano-Reggiano cheese.

'The most important thing for us is that the clients are happy. Happy at the table and happy when they leave'

From an early age, their son Giovanni contributed to the family business, and when he got married, his wife Bruna also helped out in the kitchen. The restaurant gradually became more upmarket, white tablecloths and napkins appeared as the needs and expectations of their clientele changed, and in 1960, the restaurant changed it's name to Dal Pescatore.

Giovanni and Bruna's son Antonio married Nadia in 1974. The two of them travelled extensively and ate in some of the finest restaurants, and brought back ideas about comfort, presentation and service that became the catalyst for the start of the second phase in the restaurant's development. For Dal Pescatore subsequently became a restaurant – albeit family-run – of immense reputation.

Giovanni Santini is Nadia and Antonio's son ('It's easy to remember who's who in my family,' he jokes. 'One generation is Antonio, the next is Giovanni!'). He's the fourth generation of the family to be involved with the restaurant, and now works in the kitchen alongside Nadia and Bruna.

The food is firmly rooted in the Italian tradition, with antipasti and pasta courses preceding fish or meat. The care and precision with which ingredients are chosen, prepared and presented elevates the food to another level. 'We get ingredients in twice a day if we have to, says Giovanni. 'We have to transform them in such a way as to show off their flavour to the utmost. If I choose to eat a tomato I want the flavour of a great tomato, not something else.'

One thing that has never changed is the family's desire simply to make their guests happy. 'The most important thing for us is that the clients are happy. Happy at the table and happy when they leave. We're here for them and we want to be the best we can be.'

ON ORDER

Localita Runate, 17, Canneto sull'Oglio, Mantova, Lombardy, Italy

+39 37 672 3001; www.dalpescatore.com

Head chef: Nadia, Giovanni and Bruna Santini

On the menu: Tortelli di zucca – pumpkin pasta – as well as freshwater fish, in memory of the restaurant's origins

Did you know? The restaurant's cellar contains magnums of La Tache 1982 with the serial numbers 001 and 003

Top tip: Go in daylight to enjoy the beautiful gardens and minimise the chance of getting lost

Approximate cost for two: Tasting menu €165 per person, wines start at €30 per bottle

LE CINQ

Undeniably one of Paris's most high-profile restaurants, Le Cinq can be found in one of the city's most luxurious settings, the Four Seasons Hotel George V, on the western edge of the Champs-Elysées, where it has built up a reputation and two (formerly three) Michelin stars since it opened in 1999.

The mantle of executive chef of Le Cinq has most recently been passed to Eric Briffard. A talented chef by reputation (he comes from nearby Les Elysées du Vernet), Paris is waiting with baited breath to see how Briffard rises to the challenge.

Le Cinq's setting is incredibly formal: the elegant dining room was decorated by French architect Pierre-Yves Rochon to simulate a French castle. Its entrance marked by a giant flower arrangement by Jeff Leatham, the room is dressed in grey, pale pink and gold, with stucco medallions in the ceiling, and tablecloths, china and silverware that have been custom-made for the hotel to complement its design. The restaurant also has fantastic views over the hotel's courtyard and garden.

Menus traditionally draw upon classic French flavours and ingredients, so expect to see lobster from Brittany, lamb from the Pyrénées and game from

Beauce, but they are also adventurous, featuring dishes such as roast turbot with a seaweed caramel sauce; and rack of venison served with sugared chocolate almonds.

Those looking to sample Le Cinq's signature dishes should opt for the gourmet tasting menu. It offers such delights as roast Dublin Bay prawns with Bruccio cheese and liquorice, line-caught sea bass, abalones and new onions from the Cévennes region, and roast milk-fed sweetbreads cooked risotto-style with asparagus and black truffle from the Tricastin. It is finished by an amazing dessert of crystallised wild strawberries, green apple and violet granité. For an accompaniment, sommelier Thierry Hamon has an impressive 70,000 bottles to recommend in the cellar 14 metres below the restaurant.

ON ORDER

31 Avenue George V, 75008 Paris, France

+33 (0)1 4952 7000; www.fourseasons.com/paris

Head chef: *Eric Briffard*

On the menu: *Roasted milk-fed sweetbreads, asparagus and black truffle from Tricastin cooked as a risotto*

Did you know? *A staggering 9,000 flowers are flown from Amsterdam every week for Jeff Leatham's arrangements in the hotel and the restaurant*

Top tip: *Smart-casual attire is recommended for the lunch service, but the evening is more formal, so make sure you dress for the occasion*

Approximate cost for two: *The eight-course gourmet menu costs €420 for two, not including drinks*

LA MAISON TROISGROS

First opened by Jean-Baptiste and Marie Troisgros in Roanne in 1930, their original proposition of a 'small restaurant with rooms' is a far cry from the award-winning gourmet restaurant La Maison Troisgros would become under their sons Jean and Pierre in the 1950s. So enthusiastic was the brothers' love of cuisine and so advanced was their approach and technique, in fact, that the phrase 'nouvelle cuisine' was coined by the French food critics Christian Millau and Henri Gault to describe the style of French cuisine that they, along with Paul Bocuse, Michel Guérard, Roger Verge and Paul Haeberlin, pioneered at that time.

Today, La Maison Troisgros is in the hands of a third generation, and while current owners Michel and his wife Marie-Pierre have stayed true to the restaurant's traditional French style, they've also added new flavours and ingredients to the mix. The menu in particular has a noticeable influx of Italian, Asian and American influences, particularly Japanese flavours. This, says Michel, fuses perfectly with the Troisgros philosophy in its search for 'the juxtaposition of sweetness and acidity' – an extension of what the

From the kitchen
Cannelloni filled with fromage blanc and Swiss chard (serves 4)

Ingredients:

6 fromage blanc 'faisselles' (fresh cheese in mini colanders)

4 Swiss chard leaves

8 squares of fresh pasta (such as lasagne sheets) measuring 13 x 13cm

1 shallot

1 tablespoon white wine vinegar

2 tablespoon olive oil

1 tablespoon double cream

Salt and pepper

Chives, chervil and tarragon

Method:

Drain the fromage blanc of its liquid. Trim, wash and blanch the chard leaves for a few seconds in boiling salted water. Poach the pasta squares in simmering water. Cook them for three minutes and refresh them in ice water. Drain. In a bowl, mix the cheeses with the finely diced shallot. Then add the vinegar, olive oil and cream. Season with salt and pepper. Set aside in the fridge. Place the eight squares on a work surface. Cover with the chard leaves, then place a spoonful of the filling in the centre. Roll into a cannelloni shape. Place them side by side in a baking dish. Just before serving, warm the cannelloni in the oven and place two on each plate. Drizzle with olive oil and sprinkle with fresh herbs.

'Dishes perfectly combine the acidic with the savoury, the old and the new, the west and the east'

Troisgros family term their 'cuisine acidulée', which features the fruity, palate-stimulating tastes of yuzu, sudachi, kumquat, apple and other 'acidic' flavours, paired with the savoury tastes of meat, fish, and vegetables.

Veal sweetbreads, Challans duckling caramelised with ginger, apples and grapefruit; and shredded hare and its saddle with citrus fruits are just some of the dishes that combine the acidic with the savoury, the old and the new, the west and the east. But Michel's cuisine is equally influenced by local specialities, such as fresh cheeses like Michel's current favourite, Fjord ('a cross between fromage blanc and smooth yoghurt').

His style of cuisine is a convergence of many influences. From his father, Pierre, he says he learned about the techniques and flavours of vinegars, wines, hot mustards and wasabi, and the magic of spices; while from his grandmother Anna comes the simplicity of Italian cooking, the taste of tomato sauce, and the love of lemon and citrus fruits in general. Signature dishes include saddle of lamb with natural juices, balsamic vinegar and endives; pigeon mousse with juniper; and salmon with sorrel sauce. All cooked under his father Pierre's watchful eye.

'My father is not working in the kitchen any more,' says Michel, '[but he does] let me know what he thinks of new creations. He is more of a representative. And he is mostly in the vineyard in Bourgogne. He has a passion for wine… He helps give me confidence. It is like being the son of a great star. I have to accept being compared to him. Our guests are always talking about him and my uncle. But he gives me all the responsibility. If it was not like that, I would be gone.' And there is no need for Michel to 'be gone' – he is winning plenty of awards of his own, including retaining those all-important three Michelin stars.

ON ORDER

Place Jean Troisgros, 42300 Roanne, France

+33 (0)4 7771 6697; www.troisgros.fr

Head chefs: *Michel Troisgros and Florent Boivin*

On the menu: *Grilled blue lobster in a Cancalaise butter*

Did you know? *Michel and Marie-Pierre have converted an abandoned farm near Roanne into a restaurant with gîtes, which opened summer 2008*

Top tip: *Visit the website for daily changing food tips and epicurean explanations*

Approximate cost for two: *The set menu costs from €300 for two, not including wine*

EL CELLER DE CAN ROCA

One of the restaurants at the forefront of the Spanish avant-garde scene, El Celler de Can Roca is the work of three brothers: head chef Joan Roca, maitre d' and head sommelier Josep and pastry chef Jordi. A labour of love, they originally opened the restaurant in 1986, taking over the building alongside Can Roca, the decades-old bar and restaurant that is owned and run by their parents, as it was by their parents before them.

In the beginning the restaurant was housed in a tight, ill-suited space. Joan could barely turn around in the kitchen, and the décor was modest and simple. Eventually the kitchen was remodelled to suit the evolving cuisine, which had outgrown its plain country roots. In October 2007, the restaurant was finally moved 100 metres down the road to new premises, a breathtaking dining space created with natural, organic materials and an abundance of natural light. There's also a larger, state-of-the-art kitchen-lab that gives Joan and Jordi space to experiment with the 'sous-vide cuisine' (slow cooking method) and experimental desserts for which the restaurant is well known.

The brothers take pairing dishes to the right wine seriously; many dishes created as a collaboration – Josep breaking down the notes in the wine while Joan creates a dish that complements it. Youngest brother, Jordi, is equally innovative; he's become known for creating edibles to approximate the scent of perfumes like Miracle, Eternity and Treso, while Caroline Herrera by Carolina Herrera ends up on the plate as a mix of passionfruit, caramelised red berries, rose water, orange blossom water and caramel. It's a technique that has become known as 'perfume-cooking'. The result has been an exciting blend of flavours; some scary or strange (like the cigar-shaped bar of chocolate that tastes like cigar smoke), but all delicious and innovative, and well-deserving of El Celler's two Michelin stars.

ON ORDER

Can Sunyer, 48, E-17007 Girona, Spain

+34 972 222 157; www.cellercanroca.com

Head chef: *Joan Roca*

On the menu: *Jordi's extraordinary dairy dessert, featuring yogurt, candy floss and dulce de leche*

Did you know? *The wine cellar contains five small rooms, each featuring a screen showing videos of the vineyards*

Top tip: *Order the tasting menu for the full flavour of Catalonian cuisine or ask Joan to prepare you one of his 'special surprise menus' at the more-than-reasonable-price of €115 per person*

Approximate cost for two: *€190, including wine*

L'HÔTEL DE VILLE

Named the best restaurant in the world by *Gault Millau*, Philippe Rochat had a lot to live up to when he inherited the award-winning L'Hôtel de Ville restaurant just outside of Lausanne in Switzerland from his mentor (and many say the best chef of his time) Frédy Girardet in 1996. But Rochat has managed to live up to it and more, retaining its three Michelin stars and building on Girardet's philosophy of fresh, seasonal produce to the extent that the menu changes constantly as new ingredients come into season and others fall out. 'I take the best produce of Europe and use it in season. What I cook is what I myself want to eat,' he says.

Ever the perfectionist (a trait he is also said to have learned from his mentor), Rochat rarely leaves the kitchen, choosing instead to be present for every service he can, so that he can check each dish out. It's that meticulous attention to detail that has brought gourmands from all over the world to the tiny town of Crissier to what was formerly its town hall (hence its name L'Hôtel de Ville).

But the disciple is no mere imitator of his master. Located within an old stone house in the French-speaking canton of Vaud, Rochat's menu is unashamedly French in inspiration, as are his roots. With dishes such as roast duck with a Brouilly sauce, quality of preparation and blending of flavours come as standard with Rochat's cuisine, but he has modernised the dishes as well with bold, expert touches. And he's not afraid to take chances: 'It's not enough to look, you have to really see the product. That's what's important and then always improve on it. No need to add a multitude of ingredients to refine the product. Three flavours per dish are sufficient,' he says.

ON ORDER

Rue d'Yverdon 1, 1023 Crissier (VD), Switzerland

+41 21 634 0505; www.philippe-rochat.ch

Head chefs: *Philippe Rochat and Benoît Violier*

On the menu: *Crispy langoustine with violet artichoke; egg with white truffles from Alba and hare à la royale*

Did you know? *When Rochat isn't in the kitchen, he's found enjoying the great outdoors, cross-country skiing in the winter and cycling in the summer*

Top tip: *Opt for the duck and it will be carved at the table by Louis Villeneuve, the maitre d' and the restaurant's second-in-command for the last 30 years. Villeneuve has taken the carving of ducks to an art form, having served over 30,000 at the restaurant*

Approximate cost for two: *Expect to pay between €200 and €300 for a set menu for two people, not including wine*

HOF VAN CLEVE

Many people have remarked upon arriving at Hof van Cleve how much it still looks, from a distance, and before you spot the Porsches and Mercedes in the car park, as if it could still be a working farm. It's on a 60-metre elevation, giving it fine views over the surrounding countryside; fertile agricultural land.

It's just a half hour away from chef Peter Goossen's childhood home, Zottegem, where he grew up with parents who were good cooks and enthusiastic restaurant-goers. Hotel school was a natural step, after which, four years in Paris beckoned. He worked at the Pre Catalan and the Pavillon d'Elysée, which was, he says, 'a fantastic, key experience. I learned the foundations of cuisine as well as the routine of running a restaurant and how to spot the best produce.'

In the early 1990s, when Goossens was looking for premises of his own, Hof van Cleve came up for sale. The former farmhouse was being run as a simple steak house at the time, but prior to that it had belonged to a reclusive farmer, Mr van Cleve, who lived there until he died in 1970. It had also, because of its elevated position, been used by the Germans during World War I as a lookout point.

Hof van Cleve – Goossens kept the historical name – opened in 1992, and since then its staff – with the unnerving command of foreign languages so common in this part of the world – has been welcoming guests keen to experience a cuisine that has won international plaudits. Goossens talks about how rooted he feels to the land where he grew up and the abundant produce such fertile farmland has to offer – such as the Belgian endive, white asparagus and wild mushrooms. At the same time he's inspired by the surly North Sea, whose band of fishermen catch, he believes, some of the best produce the oceans have to offer. Sole, turbot and langoustine appear regularly on his seasonal menus. Guests can expect a warm welcome from Goossen's wife Lieve and dishes such as 'scallops from Dieppe' (smoked eel, black salsify, foie gras) and 'Ecuador chocolate' (hammam tea, tonka beans, blackcurrant).

ON ORDER

Riemegemstraat 1, 9770 Kruishoutem, Belgium

+32 (0) 9383 5848; www.hofvancleve.com

Head chef: *Peter Goossens*

On the menu: *Fillet of Danish cod with anchovy butter, spider crab, leek and sabayon of oysters*

Did you know? *Kruishoutem is the 'egg capital of Belgium'. And Peter Goossens is a judge on the TV restaurant reality show* Mijn Restaurant

Top tip: *In summer, diners can purchase a cigar from Goossens' extensive collection to enjoy outside on the terrace*

Approximate cost for two: *€340, including service but not wine*

MARTÍN BERASATEGUI

Martín Berasategui's 60-cover restaurant in Lasarte-Oria, just 6km outside of San Sebastián, has long been in the vanguard of the Basque country's cooking revolution, or at least its so-called second wave.

But for Berasategui, it's not so much a movement as a gift. 'Cooking does not belong to anyone,' he says. 'It belongs to all the people who've cooked since the remote past. The objective is to know how to interpret it.' And that is what he seeks to do in the gentle countryside of Lasarte-Oria in his own particular way.

It all started rather simply, with the Bodegón Alejandro, the restaurant that was owned and run by his mother and aunt in the old part of San Sebastián, which he took over from them in 1981. It took him five years to earn his first Michelin star for the restaurant, conscious of a desire to hone the skills that his mother had passed on to him as a child.

But it wasn't until he opened Martín Berasategui in 1993 that things really began to take off. The Michelin stars came first: number one arrived in 1994, the second in 1996 and the third in 2001. By this time, praise and accolades were also coming thick and fast (he has since earned almost every international culinary award), but Berasategui's creativity was

The best of Martín Berasategui's cuisine: the great degustation menu

2007   Lightly smoked cod with powder of hazelnuts, coffee and vanilla

1995   Mille-feuille of smoked eel, foie gras, spring onions and green apple

2007   Peach gazpacho with cockles and Txakoli

This will be followed by:

2006   Oyster with watercress, rocket leaves and apple chlorophyll; lemon grass cream with oxalis acetosella

2008   The apple and forgotten tuber plate, chip and ice-cream with mustard sandwich

2006   Scallop and sea urchin custard with soya sprout, coffee cream, cinnamon and curry

2007   Farmer's egg with beetroot and liquid herbs salad, carpaccio of Basque stew and cheese

2002   Warm vegetable hearts, salad with seafood, cream of lettuce hearts and idionised juice, with Pago de los Baldios de San Carlos olive oil

2008   Roast red mullet with crystals of soft scales, rock fish juice with saffron, black olives liquid bubble

2008   Roasted Araiz's pigeon, fresh pasta with mushrooms and spring onions, touches of truffle cream

And desserts to finish:

2008   Warm and cold of apple and roots

2008   Celery ice-cream with its sprouts and leaves, cold mango slices, beetroot and fruit compote

2008   Cold essence of basil with lime sherbet, juniper ice shavings and raw almond touches

'I propose that you allow me to seduce you in small mouthfuls'

developing too. Many of his classic dishes, the roast Dover sole with clam oil, citric fruit, black mint, dry tangerine and nut powder for instance, date back to his early days (in the case of the Dover sole, to 2001). The mille-feuille of smoked eel, foie gras, spring onions and green apple dates back even further, to 1995. Each dish is dated on his menu to show the growth and transformation in his style.

Today, his style is immediately recognisable, centred as it is around the presentation of a small (but luxurious), piece of fish or meat, paired with novel dried, liquidised, foamed or creamed components. It is a template which allows for endless fun and variation. 'I propose', he says of his 13-course tasting menu, 'that you allow me to seduce you in small mouthfuls'.

Seduce it may, but the tasting menu is also a veritable marathon, which can last for hours. Fortunately, the restaurant terrace has fantastic views of the surrounding hills and farmland, and guests are encouraged to repair there periodically for breaks during the courses. Sometimes the best is kept for last: Berasategui is considered to be one of the best Basque pastry chef so don't miss out on dessert.

However, despite all the hype, the label of molecular gastronomy and the accompanying gimmicks, Berasategui's food is, at its heart, focused on a simple and genuine attempt to be subtle and pure in its presentation of textures and flavours. So advanced is he in this goal, that his attention to detail is without comparison, and he is commonly held to be one of, if not the, world's most technically accomplished cooks. It is also this philosophy that when nurtured in proteges at his restaurant, has led to the rise of subsequent chefs such as Andoni Luis Aduriz, now of Mugaritz, and Josean Martínez Alija, currently at the Guggenheim Bilbao.

ON ORDER

Loidi Kalea 4, 20160 Lasarte-Oria, Gipuzkoa, Spain

+34 943 366 471; www.martínberasategui.com

Head chef: *Martín Berasategui*

On the menu: *Celery ice-cream with its sprouts and leaves, mango slices, beetroot and fruits compote*

Did you know? *Berasategui also runs the traditional Bodegon Alejandro, where he first started cooking as a 13-year-old boy*

Top tip: *Book for a date when Martín Berasategui will himself be in the kitchen (which is, as it happens, most of the time) and you may get to meet him – he usually does a tour of the dining room in the late evening*

Approximate cost for two: *The tasting menu (13 courses) costs €310 for two, not including wine*

NOBU

With Robert de Niro as a backer, Boris Becker frolicking in the cupboards and stars of Kate Moss's calibre regularly occupying its VIP tables, it's easy to forget that Nobu London is a world-class restaurant and not just a celebrity safe house with food.

This feted London luminary was the first European venture by acclaimed Japanese sushi chef Nobu Matsuhisa, the industrious owner of 21 restaurants, from Honolulu to Hong Kong. Opened in 1997 on the first floor of the minimalist Metropolitan Hotel, a year later it scooped a Michelin star with its Japanese and South American fusion cooking and has gone on to become a lively haunt of the rich and infamous. And much of this success has been based on Nobu's passion for food: 'I always put something special in my food – my heart.'

With a career that has taken him from a sushi bar in Tokyo to Alaska, arguably one of Nobu's most important stints abroad was working in Lima, where weaving Peruvian influences into dishes became his signature style. The presentation is exquisite and key dishes that regularly cause gasps of excitement

The drinks list

The wine list at Nobu makes for a good read – Rieslings, and Gewürztraminers feature prominently as they are best suited to this style of cooking. The restaurant also has unique cocktails such as the Saketini, made of vodka, sake, plum wine, triple sec, cranberry and grapefruit juice. Nobu also holds the exclusive rights to serve Hokusetsu sake, a premium brand which is produced on Sado Island in Japan. The different varieties have flavours that range from fresh and delicate to one with a smoky finish.

'Not only does this mean that lots of different dishes can be tasted, but this is a very social and friendly way of eating'

include the yellowtail sashimi with jalapeno and the famous black cod in miso. The menu is designed for family-style dining, which means all dishes are served in the middle of the table and guests are encouraged to share everything. 'Not only does this mean that lots of different dishes can be tasted,' says Nobu, 'but it's a very social and friendly way of eating.'

The 150-cover restaurant includes a separate sushi bar and the minimalist, chic interior has fabulous views across Hyde Park. The interiors by United Designers make subtle use of light wood and natural stone to reflect the diverse influences of Nobu's cuisine, while the purity and quality of the materials used makes a nod to traditional Japanese design.

For diners looking for something different, Nobu London also offers the Omakase ('from the heart') menu, that consists of dishes full of passion and flair, which change on a regular basis. It is this attention to detail that has led to the restaurant's huge popularity and a clientele made up mainly of loyal regulars and a mix of the general public and celebrities. The service achieves that difficult juggle of being relaxed yet slick.

Under the direction of executive chef Mark Edwards, Nobu London is still going strong, even in its 11th year. Critics may scoff, but the restaurant's food more than justifies the hype. The chefs use as much local seafood as possible in each of the Nobu restaurants, which for Edwards means Scottish salmon and scallops, Dover sole, clams, sea bass and eels. The rest is flown in from overseas, including one of the most expensive items on the menu, the sea urchin that comes in from Japan.

Each new restaurant, Edwards says, contributes new ideas to the others. 'It's like a recipe book that is always growing.' But the fundamentals of its Japanese style of cooking remain the same: freshness, quality and simplicity. 'Nothing too complicated,' he says. 'There are never more than three flavours in a dish.'

ON ORDER

The Metropolitan Hotel, 19 Old Park Lane, London W1K 1LB, UK

+44 (0)20 7447 4747; www.noburestaurants.com

Head chef: *Nobuyuki Matsuhisa and executive chef Mark Edwards*

On the menu: *New dishes, such as wagyu and foie gras gyoza, ponzu and daikon oroshi are just as tempting as that iconic black cod*

Did you know? *The Nobu London broom cupboard was where Boris Becker famously had a rendezvous with a fellow diner, which resulted in his lovechild*

Top tip: *If you drop by on the off-chance, you can add your name to a waiting list for cancellations, although this often runs to two pages – consider opting for a seat at the sushi bar instead, where they serve the full restaurant menu*

Approximate cost for two: *£140 (£70 per head), not including wine*

EL RACÓ DE CAN FABES

Formerly the site of chef-proprietor Santi Santamaria's family home (Santamaria was actually born on the premises), Can Fabes was just a simple family bistro when Santamaria began to teach himself his chosen trade here at the age of 24; he hasn't worked anywhere else since. Today, El Racó de Can Fabes (or Can Fabes as it is known for short) has become known as one of Spain's most welcoming and most culinarily challenging restaurants, and yet all Santamaria wanted to do was to interpret and emphasise the quality of the locally-sourced produce that is in abundance in the area.

'For over two centuries, the walls of Can Fabes have been part of the history of the locality,' he says. 'The cooking is nourished by the produce of the land and the specialties each season brings. We need to drink from the roots, drawing maximum benefit so that experience lays the foundations of what evolution will complement, offering the best of yesterday, today and tomorrow.'

The result is a consistently challenging, but at the same time reassuring menu with a rustic edge and

Chef's tasting menu

'True market cooking is finding seasonal produce on your plate, and that is why the vegetables speak with their own flavour. As simple as that, no more no less,' says Santi Santamaria. That's why he creates seasonal menus like the following, to tempt his guests:

Spring Set Menu

- Asparagus: both wild and farmed, in a salad with wood pigeon

- Langoustines: with warm pea vinaigrette

- Casserole: of sea urchins and 'amourettes' with beans and sardine caviar

- Garter fish: sautéed with spring onions and mange-tout in red wine

- Chalosse ox: fondant, with potatoes crushed in the mortar with herbs

- Cottage cheese: homemade

- White chocolate: with praline

- Petits fours

'What I like to do with this product in its purest state is adapt it to my preferences and adapt it to enable it to transmit pleasure'

many recognisable old favourites, such as ravioli de gambes (prawn-stuffed ravioli) and cauliflower yogurt with smoked cod caviar. In fact, if there is one thing that defines Santamaria's cuisine, it is his adherence to tradition and his obsessive reworking of classic dishes. Year-on-year, he refines and modernises the same dishes that he has been working on for the last 20 years.

'The word "renew" is beautiful,' he says. 'Based on what we put on a dish, we build an environment, we build a society. Based on how we manipulate ingredients, we're starting something. I don't use any product that is not natural, which hasn't been elaborated on by the chefs.'

For, while Santamaria may not present his food with the same scientifically-based flourishes as his contemporaries, he is still, for many, the leader in the field. He was the first Catalan chef to win three Michelin stars (which he did in 1994), and he achieved this not by following outlandish trends, but by drawing on the richness of the local produce and working and refining its flavours to perfection.

Like most Catalan restaurants, Can Fabes' menu combines sea and land, sourcing products that come from the Mediterranean coast and those from inland locales. But the menu varies depending on the season and which products are available in the farms of nearby Montseny at the time. 'We start from a product in its purest state,' he explains. 'And what I like to do with this product in its purest state is adapt it to my preferences and adapt it to enable it to transmit pleasure, without betraying what in essence is the product – so that you can recognise what you're eating, so that you don't have to go through an intellectual exercise each time you eat. I don't think every time you should have to wonder what you're eating. There's an instinctive, natural point.'

His philosophy of cuisine? 'I am a craftsman cook – my personality is shaped at Can Fabes and projected out to the world.'

ON ORDER

Sant Joan, 6 Sant Celoni 08470, Spain

+34 938 672 851; www.canfabes.com

Head chef: *Santi Santamaria and executive chef Ivan Sola*

On the menu: *Ravioli de gambes*

Did you know? *Santamaria worked originally as an industrial designer and created the two-litre bottle for Coca-Cola*

Top tip: *You can book a 'gastronomic package' to Can Fabes, including one night's accommodation, lunch at Espai Coch (its sister restaurant) and dinner at Can Fabes for €850 per person, including wine*

Approximate cost for two: *€350 for two, not including wine*

ENOTECA PINCHIORRI

On the edge of one of Italy's best-loved and most visited historical centres, Enoteca Pinchiorri has survived as a true example of what *mangiare bene* (to eat well) really means in Tuscany's capital Florence – easier said than done when you consider the tourist restaurants that surround it.

It has been awarded three stars by the Michelin Guide since 1993 and received its first Michelin star in 1982, less than a decade after it first opened its doors. A mark not simply of the standard of the cuisine, but also the love and affection invested in the restaurant by its owner and chief sommelier Giorgio Pinchiorri and his French-born wife Annie Féolde, the chef that first brought in those three Michelin stars.

Housed in an imposing 16th-century palazzo, the ambiance is unavoidably formal. The emphasis here is on refined cuisine in a harmonious setting with the kind of hand-engraved silver cutlery, porcelain crockery and crystal glasses you're almost

A world of wine

The service is presided over by Giorgio Pinchiorri, who greets all of his guests, taking them into the comfort of a welcoming lounge where they can consult the menu and enjoy an aperitif while they wait to be seated.

But Giorgio really comes into his own when the wine list is brought out. His cellar contains around 150,000 wines – the result of decades of scouring Italy and the world to find the best bottles and vintages to serve his guests. So exclusive is his cellar, in fact, that some of the top Italian wine producers select and bottle great wines exclusively for him.

If you shy away from ordering a bottle of one of its most exclusive vintages, you can also order by the glass. There is an accompanying spirits list which includes fine, rare armagnacs, cognacs and grappas with which to finish your meal.

'Every dish is a symphony in which the colours, the aromas and the presentation each have their importance'

afraid to touch. And, with its frescoed ceilings and polite requests for jackets (and ties) to be worn in its dining room, the Enoteca could appear to be stuck in something of a time warp. That, however, couldn't be further from the truth.

Supporting Féolde in the kitchen is a young and dynamic team of hard-working chefs, including Italo Bassi, Riccardo Monco and pastry chef Loretta Fanella who has recently been recruited from El Bulli. Under Féolde's direction, innovative, often surprising dishes – such as guinea fowl-stuffed double ravioli, black sesame ice-cream and pigeon risotto – pepper its carefully crafted menu, offering a modern take on what is essentially traditional Tuscan fare, albeit with a subtle French twist.

And this certainly isn't the type of cuisine that you'd find on any Tuscan table; it has been studied, crafted, reworked and then reworked again, in order to get the best out of the region's seasonal produce. If money is no object and you want to be spoiled by old-world class and sophistication, then Enoteca will not disappoint.

'Every dish is a symphony in which the colours, the aromas and the presentation each have their importance,' explains Féolde. 'It is essential to avoid distorting the taste of the ingredients'. She also wants to showcase their flavour, letting the ingredients speak for themselves in all their variety, which is why one of the Enoteca's specialties has become to prepare one ingredient in a range of different styles, revealing not only the full range of its taste and texture, but also the skill and innovation of the chefs.

It's true that with its traditional style of service, the formality of the Enoteca may not be for everyone, but don't be put off by the pomp and circumstance. With a sister restaurant recently opened in Tokyo and a consistent quality of cooking that has ensured its three Michelin stars for 15 years, the Enoteca Pinchiorri will be a force to be reckoned with on the international culinary scene for many years to come.

ON ORDER

Via Ghibellina 87, 50122 Florence, Italy

+39 (0)55 242757; www.enotecapinchiorri.com

Executive chef: *Annie Féolde and head chefs Italo Bassi and Riccardo Monco*

On the menu: *Lamb shoulder gratinated with herbs, shallots in a sweet and sour sauce and glazed potatoes*

Did you know? *Part of Enoteca Pinchiorri's wine cellar was destroyed by fire in 1992, wiping out several thousand euros worth of important wines*

Top tip: *Enoteca Pinchiorri's unique cellar contains around 150,000 bottles. If in doubt ask Giorgio Pinchiorri to recommend a vintage that suits your order*

Approximate cost for two: *€450, not including wine*

LE MEURICE

Classic, timeless and shameless Parisian luxury can be found in Le Meurice, the restaurant of the five-star Dorchester Hotel le Meurice on Paris's rue de Rivoli, overlooking the Tuilleries Gardens. The legendary venue was inspired by the Salon de la Paix at Versailles and updated in 2007 by Philippe Starck, no less. He didn't get rid of any of its opulence, however. The restaurant entrance is marked by a formidable glass door, which leads into a formal dining room that is positively dripping with mirrors, gilding, chandeliers and marble. But this old-style French elegance still somehow manages to enhance rather than detract from the experience of eating here.

Head chef, the French-born Yannick Alléno has been at the helm for the past five years, with a staff of 74 and a mission 'to reinvent gastronomic cuisine', which he does with verve in his degustation menu – so much so that legendary French chef Joël Robuchon termed it 'a successful combination of classic tradition and sensible modern style'.

From his appetiser of 'just opened' shellfish with sea urchin coral, through to his duck foie gras iodised

Desserts by Camille

Le Meurice's pastry chef, Camille Lesecq, has dessert-making in his blood; he spent most of his childhood in his uncle's pastry shop watching and learning the trade he would go on to pursue. 'I still love to take inspiration from the secrets of tiny pastry shops that I discover completely by chance,' he says. His latest creation is the pomme d'amour (love apple) that he invented for Valentine's Day. 'I am always trying to surprise', he explain. 'I want my desserts to be remembered for a long time afterwards'.

Guests can currently choose from:

- Sliced poached peaches with strawberry syrup
- Thick verbena cream and frosted pastry sticks
- Melted chocolate mousse cake
- 'Yuzu' lemon sorbet under a meringue mikado
- Seaweed biscuit
- Melted mango in whipped white egg

- Soft plum cheesecake with ginger
- Juicy pear refreshed with vanilla
- Melted chocolate cake and buttered cookies
- Crunchy cherry and sweet bellpepper pastry
- 'Espelette' pepper ice-cream, Basque cake
- Strawberries and rhubarb

'Alléno's cooking has a personality. He has a knack for being ahead of what is happening'

in sugar bread; to 'love' apple, raspberry cream with jasmine and lemon meringue, Alléno's creative use of rigorously selected raw ingredients has pushed Le Meurice to the cutting edge of French cuisine. All with a suitably sumptuous cellar to match.

Even the à la carte menu, traditionally more classical in approach, revels in its chef's dexterity. The 'chaud-froid' (hot and cold) sole with its Noilly aspic jelly, fish mousse and chopped mushrooms sautéed in butter; and the loin of veal from Corrèze flavoured with elder blossom and stuffed zucchini, tomato, onion, lettuce and potato, both manifest an attention to detail and a sense of flair not normally expected from a restaurant hotel (anywhere other than Paris), even if it is a high-class one.

'Alléno's cooking has a personality. He has a knack for being ahead of what is happening. It is all about the product,' explains Alexandre Gaudelet, the restaurant manager.

As for Alléno, he just wants everyone to enjoy the experience: 'I always think of what will please people. The goal is ensure that everyone has a good time,' he says. And, while he may have relaxed the restaurant's dress code (he is said to like the buzz of a noisy, more informal setting), the same cannot be said for his standards in the kitchen. The menu is selected on the strength of the ingredients available that day, and even popular dishes are left off the menu if the raw produce does not come up to the chef's stringent standards.

'I want to progress and perfect my work in order to offer a true gastronomic signature,' he says. 'With my team at Le Meurice, I want to affirm this wish through a cuisine that is forever more rigorous, finer, and more creative, and to pass on this quest for excellence in order to represent and promote French gastronomy.'

ON ORDER

228 rue de Rivoli, 75001 Paris, France

+33 (0)1 4458 1010; www.lemeurice.com

Head chef: *Yannick Alléno*

On the menu: *Breast of pigeon in a chocolate crust*

Did you know? *Salvador Dalí once ordered a flock of sheep to be delivered to his room at Hotel Le Meurice and proceeded to fire at them with a pistol, fortunately loaded with blanks*

Top tip: *Order the degustation menu. It's €220 each, but you'll get to enjoy nine fantastic courses including Alléno's 'cheese served in snow'*

Approximate cost for two: *€350 for two, not including wine*

VENDÔME

Though this is the first time that Swabia-born chef Joachim Wissler's Vendôme has entered the S.Pellegrino World's 50 Best Restaurants list, it is unlikely that it will be last. Wissler's innovative take on classic dishes such as dove Bresse with Treviso radicchio braised in sherry with mildly smoked potato purée and parsley; and saddle of venison with olive brittle, savoy cabbage and small orzo pasta led Vendôme to its first Michelin star in its first year of business. It collected one more in 2003 and the third in 2004.

Named after Paris's famous Place Vendôme, the restaurant is surprisingly small (the interior only has nine tables), but perfectly formed and undeniably formal. This luxury restaurant occupies part of a former nobleman's home and one of Europe's most beautiful Baroque castles, the glorious five-star Grandhotel Schloss Bensberg in Bergisch Gladbach, near Cologne. And, it's not just the stunning views of Cologne Cathedral that brings tourists here.

Renovated in 2007, Vendôme uses zebrano wood, travertine granite, carved crown moulding and stained

Wined and dined

Vendôme's wine list, featuring over 900 different wines, meets the exacting standards of world-class wine enthusiasts, offering both classic wines and many well-kept secrets. The sommelier, Romana Echensperger, used to work at the renowned hotel Königshof in Munich and is extremely adroit at matching wines with dishes.

'My aim is to work out the flavour of the product and to cook in a reasoned and pure way – every ingredient has to play a main part'

glass to enhance the historic atmosphere. The effect is a contemporary yet timeless elegance that complements Wissler's straightforward classic French haute cuisine. This is the chef, after all, that trained in the kitchen of Harald Wohlfahrt in Die Schwarzwaldstube (p142) in the Black Forest in the early 1980s, so he knows a thing or two about the power of flavour.

This experience and his time at the Marcobrunn Restaurant in Erbach helped Wissler to establish the style that has led him to worldwide acclaim: his classic but imaginative concoctions blend refinement with just the right splash of daring, while the quality of the ingredients remains paramount. Wissler is a chef that knows how to emotionally move his guests.

Of his dishes, Wissler says: 'My aim is to work out the flavour of the product and to cook in a reasoned and pure way. Every ingredient has to play a main part in the composition that I make.' Signature dishes include marmorated mascarpone ravioli with parsley spinach, bonded Jabugo Bellotta ham juice and old balsamico, followed by white peach with curry cream, raspberry coulis, souffled polenta and pine nut ice-cream. 'To not mince our words, Joachim Wissler is a genius of flavour,' said Lo Mejor de la Gastronomia restaurant guide.

Vendôme has two menus to choose from – a tasting menu and a main menu. The tasting menu breaks down into a small and a large version depending on your appetite, and holds delights such as fillet of red mullet with cep couscous, tomatoes and a coconut and coriander foam. The main menu, on the other hand, has around 18 creations to mull over, with dishes – such as Bretonian lobster with caramelised pomelo and spiced yoghurt; or Treviso radicchio ravioli with Périgord truffles in a Parmesan velouté – that taste even better than they sound.

Sommelier Romana Echensperger adds the finishing touches; her wine selection stretches from costly classics to insider's tips – in short, the right wine for every occasion.

ON ORDER

Grandhotel Schloss Bensberg, Kadettenstrasse, 51429 Bergisch Gladbach, Germany

+49 (0)220 4420; www.schlossbensberg.com

Head chef: *Joachim Wissler*

On the menu: *Skate wing with green olive vegetables, glasswort tips and caper sauce*

Did you know? *The South Korean football team stayed at Schloss Bensberg during the World Cup 2006, but brought their own chef with them*

Top tip: *Make sure your plan your visit carefully as the restaurant is closed on Mondays and Tuesdays. It is open Wednesday to Sunday from noon to 2pm, and 7pm to 9pm*

Approximate cost for two: *€220 for two, not including wine*

DIE SCHWARZ-WALDSTUBE

As its name suggests, Die Schwarzwaldstube can be found in one of Germany's most beautiful landscapes, the Black Forest, although this may seem a little out of the way for an award-winning restaurant – particularly when you consider that visitors originally came to Heiner and Renate Finkbeiners' Hotel Traube Tonbach for the mountain sports rather than for its cuisine.

Chef Harald Wohlfahrt has changed all of that, however, during nearly 30 years behind the restaurant stove. So precise is his approach to the local ingredients (he is even said to cook with tweezers) that he has logged up three Michelin stars and scored 19/20 in the annual *Gault Millau* guide – and has no plans to slow down. And why should he? Amid panoramic views over the Black Forest meadows, guests rave about his artful use of the region's local ingredients, particularly its game, fruit, berries and mushrooms, while critics heap praise on his innovative take on regional cuisine.

The influence of time spent training with Alain Chapel near Lyon can be seen in the French flavour of Wohlfahrt's cuisine. He is also one of the few to be able to effortlessly combine traditional French ingredients with Asian flavours to almost magical effect, as he has shown with his steamed lobster on a bed of leeks with a lemongrass sauce, and his red mullet with melon chutney and Thai curry sauce.

The fine dining is further enhanced by the venue: a warm, peaceful building with high timbered ceilings, stocky oak dining chairs and large panoramic windows that allow guests to look across the meadows and towards the forest – while the food is enjoyably hearty and rich, there's plenty of green and pleasant land in which to work up an appetite.

ON ORDER

Hotel Traube Tonbach, 72270 Baiersbronn im Schwarzwald, Germany

+49 (0)7442 492665; www.traube-tonbach.de

Head chef: *Harald Wohlfahrt*

On the menu: *Steamed lobster on a bed of leeks with a lemongrass sauce*

Did you know? *Wohlfahrt's take on space food will be feeding the astronauts on the International Space Station. The menu, being introduced in March 2009, includes braised calf's cheeks, plum compote with star anise and potato soup with blood sausage*

Top tip: *The Hotel Traube Tonbach has four restaurants, so make sure you book the right one by asking specifically for Die Schwarzwaldstube or Wohlfahrt*

Approximate cost for two: *Menus cost from €280 to €360 for two, not including wine*

LE CALANDRE

When a restaurant offers a bottle of 1995 Dom Pérignon at around £5,750 on its vast wine list, you can rest assured that you're dealing with real quality. That's certainly the case at Le Calandre, a culinary delight located in the largely inconspicuous Italian village of Sarmeola di Rubano, outside Padua, near Venice.

Firmly a family business, current head chef Massimiliano and his brother Raffaele (front-of-house) are fifth in a line of great chefs and restaurateurs. Massimiliano worked at Alfredo Chiocchetti's restaurant Ja Navalge in Moena, Marc Veyrat's Auberge de l'Eridan in Veyrier du Lac d'Annecy and at Michel Guérard's Les Prés d'Eugénie in Eugénie les Bains before returning to Le Calandre to join his brother in 1993. His one desire was to maintain the Michelin star earned there with his mother.

He did that and much more, bringing in the second Michelin star in 1996, making him the youngest chef ever to be awarded two stars at the time. A third Michelin star followed in 2002 (still the youngest to have received the accolade). So much buzz surrounded the occasion that he was christened 'the Mozart of the kitchen' by journalist Paolo Marchi.

Il Calandrino

Adjoining the restaurant is Le Calandre's bar and pastry shop, Il Calandrino. This is the domain of Raffaele and Massimiliano's mother Rita, who works from seven in the morning until midnight, baking delicious pastries, mousses, brioches, croissants and panetonni – all without preservatives and using natural yeasts.

The brothers also have a food shop, In.gredienti, which sells Italian delicacies, such as cheese, salami, extra virgin olive oil, pasta and wine.

'It's not enough for me just to taste the raw fillet – I need to know the animal's origin in order to pin down the flavour of the herbs it ate'

And while Massimiliano (or Max as he is often known) concentrates on the cuisine, Raffaele is busy in the wine cellar matching vintages to his guests' palates. His list includes over 1,500 labels, stored in two cellars: one for Italian wines, the other for French. He is always on hand to suggest a variety that will match the dishes on Massimiliano's Grand Classics or In.gredienti tasting menus.

Classic dishes include such delights as spaghetti with squid liver, oil and spicy pepper; hand-chopped beef lightly seasoned with a truffled egg sauce, served on a bark dish or cutting board with dressed wholewheat bread; cappuccino di seppie al nero (a cream of potato soup with squid ink); and Gorgonzola ice-cream with pepper and powder of raspberries. Others, such as 'The Gardening', make big waves for other reasons – this dish offers delicate Piemontese beef, chopped, ground and seasoned, to be eaten by hand in its pure state (the only additional flavours are provided by the edible flowers and powdered fruits that decorate the plate). Another, risotto allo zafferano con polvere di liquirizia (saffron risotto with liquorice powder) offers an almost unrecognisable take on an Italian classic.

Massimiliano is a chef guided by instincts: 'I create dishes first in my head,' he says, before he transforms his visions from head to plate. 'I have to know where a piece of meat comes from. It's not enough for me just to taste the raw fillet – I need to know the animal's origin in order to pin down the flavour of the herbs it ate. Why? So I can use the same herbs when cooking it. This is a fundamental rule of my cooking. If a meal smells good people will want to taste it.'

ON ORDER

Via Liguria 1, 35030 Sarmeola di Rubano, Padova, Italy

+39 (0)4 963 0303; www.alajmo.it

Head chef: *Massimiliano Alajmo*

On the menu: *Hand-chopped beef lightly seasoned with a truffled egg sauce, served on a bark dish or cutting board with dressed wholewheat bread*

Did you know? *Alajmo has created a new version of his il Gioccolato (gioco al cioccolato, a game with chocolate) every year since 2003*

Top tip: *For the latest advances in Massimiliano's cuisine, opt for the tasting menu*

Approximate cost for two: *The set menu of Le Calandre's classic dishes costs €380 for two, not including wine*

CHEZ PANISSE

Chez Panisse opened its doors in 1971 in bohemian Berkeley, California, when Alice Waters and an assortment of 'idealistic' friends decided to create an eatery in which the guests would feel as if they were having a dinner party at home. She chose to name her friendly, neighbourhood bistro after a character in Marcel Pagnol's 1930's trilogy of books (*Marius*, *Fanny* and *Cesar*), and the restaurant (downstairs, by reservation only) and café (upstairs, reservations recommended) remain to this day a homage to the sentiment, comedy and informality of these classic books (and films).

Cafe Panisse's single fixed-price menus change daily to reflect not only what was found in the marketplace that morning, but also Alice's desire to provide ecologically and ethically-sound cuisine. Organic ingredients, meticulously sourced from a network of over 60 local suppliers, are allowed to flourish in no-nonsense dishes, such as grilled and braised farm pork with Muscat sauce, potato purée and chanterelles.

'We are convinced that the best-tasting food is organically grown and harvested in ways that are ecologically sound, by people who are taking care of the land for future generations,' she says. 'The quest

Chez Panisse Foundation

In 1996, Alice Waters, pioneering cook, restaurateur and food activist, created the Chez Panisse Foundation to celebrate the 25th anniversary of her restaurant, Chez Panisse.

The foundation envisions a nationwide public school curriculum at all levels that includes hands-on experiences in school kitchens, gardens and lunchrooms. It believed that this curriculum will inspire students to choose healthy food and help them understand the impact of their choices on their health, the health of their communities and the planet.

Pointing to the mass consumer culture that is creating an unprecedented crisis of diet-related disease among the US nation's youth, the foundation is also lobbying for a school lunch system that will provide delicious, healthy, freshly prepared meals for all of students; much as Jamie Oliver has done in the UK. 'To create real change in students' eating habits, we must rethink their education and experiences with food, beginning with their experiences at school,' says Waters.

One groundbreaking model was established in Berkeley itself via the Edible Schoolyard – a working garden, kitchen and dining classroom that provides experiential learning about food.

For more information, visit www.chezpanissefoundation.org

'*Organic ingredients, meticulously sourced from a network of over 60 local suppliers, are allowed to flourish in no-nonsense dishes, such as grilled and braised farm pork with Muscat sauce...*'

for such ingredients has largely determined the restaurant's cuisine. [We want] diners to partake of the immediacy and excitement of vegetables just out of the garden, fruit right off the branch and fish straight out of the sea.'

Alice is a strong advocate for farmers' markets and for sound and sustainable agriculture. Local, seasonal and sustainable, the touchstones of so many restaurants around the world today, were firmly on Chez Panisse's agenda from day one and they still inform the menu today. 'There is probably no restaurateur in America who has done more for the farmers' market movement than Alice Waters,' said the *Los Angeles Times*.

'A good kitchen respects its sources, chooses ingredients that are sound, seasonal, local when possible, and appropriate to the event. Garnish and presentation play supplemental roles, not principal ones. Respect for traditions, both artisanal and sophisticated, is equal to respect for inventiveness and improvisation,' says Waters. 'We see farming, foraging, cooking and table service as an unbroken sequence, like food and wine, accommodation and nourishment. Remaining aware of the garden and the farm while at the table, we cannot ignore threats to either end of the sequence.'

And it's not just in the kitchen of Chez Panisse that Waters creates food to influence change. In 1996, in celebration of the restaurant's 25th anniversary, she created the Chez Panisse Foundation to help underwrite cultural and educational programmes such as the one at the Edible Schoolyard (see left) to demonstrate the transformative power of growing, cooking and sharing food, particularly among schoolchildren.

ON ORDER

1517 Shattuck Avenue, Berkeley, CA 94709-1516, USA

+1 (1)510 548 5525; www.chezpanisse.com

Head chef: *Jean-Pierre Moullé and David Tanis*

On the menu: *James Ranch lamb's tongue vinaigrette with leeks, capers and parsley*

Did you know? *Alice Waters sells her own brand of breakfast cereal called Café Fanny Organic Granola*

Top tip: *Monday night menus are generally simpler and more rustic or regional than other evenings, whereas Friday and Saturday night menus are more elaborate, hence the differences in cost*

Approximate cost for two: *A meal for two costs $130 on Mondays, $150 from Tuesdays to Thursdays and $180 on Fridays and Saturdays, not including wine*

CHARLIE TROTTER'S

Charlie Trotter insists that there are no signature dishes on the menu at his eponymous Chicago restaurant. In fact, he maintains that no dish is likely to be prepared the same way twice. He calls it 'spontaneous cuisine… an evolution of ideas.' And while the food is heavily influenced by Western European tradition, he says: 'It's certainly not classical cuisine, because there's just as much influence from the Orient. There's an Asian minimalism that runs throughout.'

It wasn't easy at first to convince a public used to a predictability in their restaurants, that the daily changing menu was a good idea. Trotter recalls an early reviewer who wanted to check the dishes he was planning on mentioning would still be on the menu in four weeks when his review came out. 'I said: "They're not on the menu now and you only ate here two nights ago", and he said: "What!" because it was such a novelty back then.'

The Charlie Trotter Culinary Education Foundation

The figure who most impressed Trotter during his wide reading around the subject of food and cooking was Fernand Point (author of *Ma Gastronomie*), especially his sense of generosity, which resonated with Trotter's own philanthropic nature.

In 1999 he founded the Charlie Trotter Culinary Education Foundation, which has raised almost $2 million to date, half of which have been given out in the form of grants and scholarships to people who would not otherwise be able to attend culinary school. The remaining money is invested in the Foundation's long-term future. Trotter was honoured for this work by President Bush, and in 2005 he was named Humanitarian of the Year by the International Association of Culinary Professionals.

In addition to this work, Charlie Trotter himself underwrites what he refers to as his 'Excellence Program'. Two or three times a week, students from public high schools in Chicago come to the restaurant and eat – free of charge – a multi-course tasting menu. The students – who might be honours students sent here as a reward, or problem students lacking motivation – get a brief tour of the restaurant before they're seated in the studio kitchen for their meal. During the meal, staff talk to the students about what they do to pursue excellence and how they motivate and set standards for themselves. It's hoped the students will be inspired to achieve their own goals. 'If we can let these folks walk out with two or three ideas about life and about how to motivate themselves, then we've accomplished our goal,' says Trotter.

'It's important to learn how to think. You can always cook'

But you won't necessarily see high-concept food on Trotter's menus, because he prefers to create dishes based on combinations that are at least partly familiar to the diner. 'I like the idea of devising dishes with an element of recognisability, a combination you might have seen before, but never put together this way.'

Wine is a huge part of the restaurant. Bottles are housed in temperature- and humidity-controlled cellars lined with custom-built redwood shelves. The restaurant's cellars contain no fewer than 20 vintages of Penfolds 'Grange', Chateaux d'Yquem dating from 1845 and 1857, and a magnum of Romanee Conti from 1945. As a result, the kitchen produces what Trotter terms 'wine-friendly' dishes – that is, ones without a lot of heat, spice or acidity.

Trotter did not come from a family that was particularly interested in food. His own interest developed thanks to a college roommate who was an avid cook and who would prepare various courses for his friends to taste. Mid-way through college (at the University of Wisconsin) Trotter decided to take a year off and read every book he could, including cookbooks. To make a living during this time he took a job as a waiter. When he returned to college, he began cooking again and catering for small parties. After graduating, he travelled around the US and Europe, eating at the finest restaurants in order to find out what those considered 'the best' were really like.

He returned to the States and worked under Gordon Sinclair at Chicago restaurant Sinclair's, along with chefs including Norman Van Aken of Norman's in Orlando, Florida and Carrie Nahabedian of Naha, Chicago. He later began to cook for dinner parties (using the tasting menu format) for friends of his family. After doing this successfully for just over a year, he decided to open Charlie Trotter's with his now deceased father, Bob Trotter, as his partner.

Trotter often advises young people keen to cook for a living to first 'study something useful in liberal arts or humanities. They need to learn how to think critically, how to argue opposing ideas. It is important for them to learn how to think. You can always cook.'

ON ORDER

816 West Armitage, Chicago, Illinois 60614, USA

+1 (1) 773 248 6228; www.charlietrotters.com

Head chef: *Charlie Trotter and chef de cuisine Matthias Merges*

On the menu: *A seasonal selection that changes daily*

Did you know? *Charlie Trotter has received the IACP 'Humanitarian of the Year' award, Share-Our-Strength's 'Most Sustainable Chef' and the Global Gastronomy 'Green' Award from the White Guild in Europe*

Top tip: *For a taste of Trotter's without the price tag, you can also sample the restaurant's gourmet cuisine at Trotter's to Go nearby in Lincoln Park*

Approximate cost for two: *Fixed-price menus start from around $180 for two, wine from $40 a bottle*

CHEZ DOMINIQUE

'It's a cliché maybe, but for me it's all about the ingredients,' says Hans Välimäki, chef-owner of Helsinki restaurant Chez Dominique. 'I've been surrounded by this amazing produce all my life. I'm like a kid in a candy store sometimes! We get a lot of light in summer, so all the fruits and vegetables taste sweeter – we also have great fish and game, it's all exciting.' Välimäki has every right to be excited – his restaurant is considered the best in Finland and its young chef (he's not yet 40) is cooking at the top of his game, using Nordic ingredients and French technique to create dazzling multi-course table menus that have been drawing an eclectic and enthusiastic crowd since the restaurant opened 10 years ago. Now on a larger site, with 50 covers (the previous site had only 26 or so), the space is starkly white but beautiful – owing a lot to a clean, Scandinavian aesthetic.

Dishes such as his Anjou pigeon show the classic side of his art; it's a pigeon prepared three ways. First a confit of the legs, then a consommé using the bones, and finally a rolled, stuffed breast. 'We've basically

been working on this dish for the past 10 years,' says Välimäki. 'Of course, some dishes we tried we'll never do again, we still laugh about some of those…'

Välimäki had what he describes as a 'traditional upbringing'. He remembers foraging for mushrooms as a child with his grandmother. And now, too, he says that hunting for wild game is enjoying a renaissance, especially among young chefs: 'Ten or 15 years ago nobody wanted to do it, but now we're real men!'

He admits that there's a certain confusion as to what actually constitutes Finnish cuisine but says: 'Our cooking is always evolving. We don't have a rich wine culture, but we do have great ingredients.'

ON ORDER

Rikhardinkatu 4, 00130 Helsinki, Finland

+358 (0)9 612 7393; www.chezdominique.fi

Head chef: *Hans Välimäki*

On the menu: *Anjou pigeon with duck foie gras, coco pastilla and Madeira sauce*

Watch out for: *The snowball – a winter-fresh 'snowball' filled with mint and berries*

Top tip: *July is the best month to visit Helsinki; the weather is at its warmest and there are around 19 hours of daylight to enjoy*

Approximate cost for two: *Tasting menus start at €95 for four courses (add another €80 for wines) and go up to €139 for the full degustation menu (add another €128 for wines)*

D.O.M.

Brazilian chef (and former DJ) Alex Atala ran three-star-Michelin eateries in both Belgium and France, including the late Bernard Loiseau's Hotel de la Côte-d'Or, before returning to Brazil to open D.O.M. in São Paulo in 1999. Building on his experiences in those kitchens, everything at D.O.M. has been designed to be just-so, from the work of architect Ruy Ohtake and landscaper Gilberto Elkis on the venue to Atala's mission to create a 'tribute to old and new ingredients' in every dish, which he does by transforming Brazilian dishes and ingredients using French and Italian techniques. The setting befits the quality of the food: the striking interior includes a five-metre-high wood door and huge striped wall hangings created by artist Ricky Castro.

But for Atala, it's also about putting something back. Born in the neighbourhood of Mooca in São Paulo, from a middle-class family of Palestinian origin, Atala knows all too well the need for support and regeneration in the city and country. By supporting the region's ingredients and its culture, he hopes not only to raise their profile around the world, but also to preserve the environment and help the people that live within it. 'If I can [promote] the Brazilian cuisine as I wish to do, communities may be benefited in turn,' he says.

And promote that cuisine and its ingredients he does. Atala is the first Latin-American chef to teach in the prestigious French school, Le Cordon Bleu, in Paris. He also set up a Brazilian Festival of Gastronomy at both the Payard Pâtisserie and the Bistrô in New York (he flew in ingredients from Brazil specially for the occasion).

'It's time to redesign the gastronomic map,' he says, referring to the dominance in Brazil of French chefs in the 1980s, so he creates tasting menus to do just that (sometimes with up to 20 courses), which include everything from codfish brandade in a black bean reduction; filhote (a type of catfish) in a manioc (cassava) crust, and banana ravioli with passion fruit sauce and tangerine sorbet.

ON ORDER

Rua Barão de Capanema, 549 Jardins,
São Paulo 01411-01, Brazil

+55 11 3088 0761; www.domrestaurante.com.br

Head chef: *Alex Atala and sous chef Geovane Carneiro*

On the menu: *Codfish brandade in a black bean reduction*

Did you know? *The acronym DOM comes from the Latin 'Deo optimo maximo', meaning 'to the greatest and best God'*

Top tip: *Atala recommends one other restaurant in Brazil, the Là em Casa Restaurant under chef Paulo Martins in Pará (Estação das Docas, G2 lj.4, Belém, Pará, +55 91 3212 5588)*

Approximate cost for two: *R$400, including wine*

DANIEL

Lyon-born Daniel Boulud's flagship New York restaurant, on Manhattan's Upper East Side, delivers, in every possible way, the French chef's ongoing ambition of offering his guests 'a dining experience that awakens all the senses'. In a grand neo-Renaissance-style dining room (soon to be revamped by renowned designer Adam Tihany), Boulud's imaginative French cuisine celebrates seasonal ingredients, indulging diners with dishes that include slow-baked striped bass with black truffle, artichoke and Satur Farms mâche salad; spiced bosc pear with Vietnamese cinnamon, Pinot Noir gelée and Poire William sorbet; and Maine sea scallops layered with black truffle in golden puff-pastry.

Boulud has a veritable army of talent working under him at Daniel: from executive chef Jean François Bruel and pastry chef Dominique Ansel to their team of over 40 cooks and sous chefs. Together, they work in a 370-metre-square state-of-the-art kitchen that was designed by Daniel Boulud himself, using cutting-edge kitchen equipment that was created especially for the restaurant to complement his techniques. A Labresse-Girardon rotisserie oven, for example, enables the kitchen to turn out sumptuous roasts basted in their

The wine cellar

Daniel's wine list spans 15 countries and comprises over 1,500 bottles that have been carefully selected by chef-sommelier Philippe Marchal. Whether you'd prefer to play safe on a $30 bottle of 1999 Château Camplazens 'La Garrigue' Coteaux du Languedoc, or can stump up the $10,000 needed for a bottle of Romanée Conti 1990, there is something for everyone (fortunately, most of it reasonably priced) in this treasure trove of international wine.

'In the life of a chef you don't create too many signature dishes. You really become known for just a few'

own juices. He is so meticulous, the story goes, that he can't stand to see a detail out of place. He definitely has his own way of doing thigs, which is why he had his kitchen equipment designed especially for him.

And yet this French exile is the very embodiment of the successful marriage between the traditional French approach to seasonal cooking and the warm and welcoming American approach to service. For while raised on all things seasonal and culinary on a farm outside of Lyon and trained by renowned French chefs – and despite being a finalist in France's competition for Best Culinary Apprentice when he was 15 – it was in the US that things really began to take off for Boulud.

This pinpoints his breakthrough to a signature dish created for New York's Le Cirque, where he worked on first arriving in the US. The 'sea scallops black tie' (a black and white dish of scallops with black truffles) 'was an instant classic that got big raves,' he says. 'It's interesting, in the life of a chef you don't create too many signature dishes. You really become known for just a few.'

At Daniel, what he is best known for is his seasonal menu: in the winter months, black truffles from Périgord appear in dishes such as roasted squab stuffed with foie gras, winter vegetables and chestnuts, while spring is announced with the arrival of asparagus, morels and delicate peas, including his celebrated asparagus, lobster and artichoke salad with fresh hearts of palm and Meyer lemon dressing.

During the summer, fragrant tomatoes, chanterelles and local sweetcorn take pride of place, Boulud emphasising their compelling flavour in his chilled summer tomato gelée with opal basil, peekytoe crabmeat and spicy avocado. His roasted tuna with country bacon, chanterelles and truffled beef jus also makes an appearance when the heat is on. Finally, in autumn, it is the fragrant, earthy white truffles of northern Italy that inspire him as he shaves them over his luxuriant risotto with porcini, or in a dish of braised turnips stuffed with pigs feet and mushrooms.

ON ORDER

60 East 65th Street, New York, NY 10065, USA

+1 (1) 212 288 0033; www.danielnyc.com

Head chef-owner: *Daniel Boulud and executive chef Jean François Bruel*

On the menu: *Cassolette of Louisiana crayfish with glazed cockscomb tempura porcini*

Did you know? *A board member of Citymeals-on-Wheels, a charity that prepares and delivers meals to New York's elderly, Boulud received a Culinary Humanitarian Award from the UN in 2007*

Top tip: *Look out for wine-tasting events at the venue with specially crafted pairing menus on offer*

Approximate cost for two: *The three-course prix-fixe menu costs $210 for two with an additional cost for wine pairings of $60 each, the six-course seasonal tasting menu is $175 per person with $95 for wine pairings, and the eight-course seasonal tasting menu is $195 each, plus $110 for wine*

OUD SLUIS

'The evolution of the kitchen will never stop,' says chef-proprietor Sergio Herman of his restaurant Oud Sluis, located in a charming Dutch market town on The Netherlands' Zeeland coast. 'Each day we are busy perfecting the performance of the previous day. Concessions are no longer made. A lot of time and energy is spent in the Oud Sluis kitchen in the quest for originality.'

It is this quest which has led Herman to three Michelin stars and a concept of cooking that he has termed 'culinary entertainment' and that he explains as the 'skillful playing' with textures, temperatures and presentations in order to showcase one ingredient in a variety of styles. A classic example of this is his Zeeland oysters, which are served in six different styles in the same dish.

The restaurant Oud Sluis is a small venue (with only 40 covers between the two dining rooms), but this suits Herman perfectly. For him, the restaurant is 'one big culinary experiment' and he seems to thrive on the spontaneous, enthusiastic and challenging nature of the cuisine, rather than the turnover it generates. It is perhaps not that surprising to discover that Herman trained under Ferran Adrià of El Bulli.

of El Bulli. And yet, his approach to Oud Sluis is different and distinctively Dutch with an Oriental twist, so expect to see unique combinations, such as oysters with kaffir lime and beer, and butternut cream with langoustine tempura.

But Herman's cuisine also draws on Dutch culinary heritage. It helps that local ingredients are so abundant, particularly seafood: langoustine, scallops, mussels, turbot and sole all take pride of place on his à la carte and 'Feeling and Taste' set menus.

ON ORDER

Beestenmarkt 2, 4524 EA Sluis, The Netherlands

+31 (0)117 461 269; www.oudsluis.nl

Head chef: *Sergio Herman*

On the menu: *Chocolate zen garden*

Did you know? *Oud Sluis now has two rooms that you can stay in*

Top tip: *It's actually easier to get to the restaurant from Belgium – Oud Sluis is only a 20-minute taxi ride from Bruges*

Approximate cost for two: *The 'Feeling and Taste' four-course menu costs €240 for two, not including wine. There's also a three-course lunch menu (€130 for two) and a 'Père et Fils' menu (€320 for two)*

RISTORANTE CRACCO

This Michelin two-star restaurant is located in central Milan next to the Milanese institution, Peck food store, and used to be a joint venture when it was known as Ristorante Cracco-Peck. Run then, as it is now, by superchef Carlo Cracco, it has built its name on its innovative twists on classic Milanese cuisine, particularly its risotto. With the likes of buffalo mozzarella-crusted oyster with pepper cream, and salad of puntarelle rice, mortadella and black tartufo on its menu and an elegant setting that was given a new lease of life by architects Gian Maria and Roberto Beretta in 2007, Ristorante Cracco has firmly established itself on the Italian culinary scene.

Cracco has an impressive pedigree. He worked as a young chef for Alain Ducasse in Monaco, and under Italy's great chef Gualtiero Marchesi (considered the inventor of Italian 'modern cuisine' and owner of the first Italian restaurant to be awarded three Michelin stars), as well as at Florence's Enoteca Pinchiorri and their satellite-restaurant in Tokyo. All these influences

The squaring of the egg

TV chef Delia Smith may have shocked the UK public in 1998 when she released a cookbook teaching culinary philistines how to boil an egg, but she's not the only chef to have become known for a love of eggs. In 2002, Carlo Cracco released his book, *The Squaring of the Egg*, which has lifted the 'poor and simple' ingredient to the position of king of the table with four astounding recipes: marinated egg yolk with white asparagus and fresh almonds; marinated egg yolk with barley white omelette and Sichuan pepper (pictured right); potato soup with dried capers and grated egg; and marinated egg yolk with sepia and glacialis.

'My dishes are always different, because to me it is important to constantly exalt cuisine in all its nuances'

can be seen in Cracco's intelligent approach to textures and flavours, which is not to say that he doesn't have his own clear and unique style.

It's an experimental approach that is driven by a chef's search for perfection. 'On the menu there are always dishes with different consistencies,' Cracco says. 'For example, we bake minced potatoes which produce crackling sounds. It's like eating paper, because they are prepared in such a way that when you chew them you blend them together again. It is all a game of calibrated structures and consistencies. Menus are conceived in such a way that they always have an alternation of consistencies and colours. If one of the courses on the menu is fried, there won't be another fried course. The same goes for sight and taste. If one of the dishes has tomato in it, there will be no other dish with tomato.'

But, above all, Cracco is driven by the desire to educate his customers in the unique qualities of Italian, particularly Milanese, cooking. 'My dishes are always different,' he explains. 'Not because what I've done before isn't good enough, but because to me it is important to constantly exalt cuisine in all its nuances. Italian cuisine is an inexhaustible source of variation and special garnishing. Abroad, Italian cuisine is all about spaghetti, tiramisu and mozzarella. When people come from abroad they are surprised and ask: "Is this Italian cuisine?"' Ristorante Cracco proves that there is so much more to experience, and provides the wine to match from its collection of 1,800 labels.

Apart from its two main dining rooms and a private room for more intimate occasions, Ristorante Cracco also has a chef's table (for two) in the kitchen itself. Book this and you'll get to see Cracco at work on the dishes for which he has become known: marrow cooked on a hot plate until translucent, risottos cooked to perfection and a personal love for eggs (he has even released a book called *The Squaring of the Egg*), which has led him to develop a system of marinating egg yolks – up to three days for certain dishes.

ON ORDER

Via Victor Hugo 4, 20123 Milan, Italy

+39 02 876 774

Head chef: *Carlo Cracco*

On the menu: *Risotto of Sichuan pepper, ginger and anchovies*

Did you know? *Cracco was educated at Scuola Alberghiera, choosing to learn his trade there simply because he liked the hotel management school's purple building*

Top tip: *Order one of Carlo Cracco's speciality white truffle dishes and risottos*

Approximate cost for two: *Guests can choose between two set menus or the à la carte list. Expect to pay from €260 for two, not including wine*

ASADOR ETXEBARRI

In contrast to the high-tech forms of modern cooking that dominate much of this list, Asador Etxebarri is practically backwards. Not only is chef-proprietor Victor Arguinzoniz self-taught, but his entire menu is produced via 'the world's oldest form of cooking' – the charcoal grill. What is even more surprising, however, is how he has elevated what he calls 'primitive cooking' to such skill and renown. *Time* magazine said the restaurant had produced the 'best steak ever', while Neil Perry of Rockpool (fish) has said it provided inspiration for his bar and grill in Melbourne.

For Arguinzoniz doesn't simply throw his raw ingredients on to the barbecue, douse them in sauces and wait until they char; he has created a whole method of cooking on a grill that starts with the charcoal that is used to fire it. Each a secret recipe of wood from neighbouring trees, he has a charcoal for each ingredient that he cooks: oak for delicate ingredients like seafood and mushrooms; smoky

How to get there

Asador Etxebarri isn't the most complicated restaurant to get to on this list, but it's certainly not the easiest. Less than an hour's drive from Bilbao, it can be found by following the A8 east from the city (signposted for Donostia/San Sebastián) for 32km until the junction 17 (marked Durango). From there you need to take the N-634 east for 2.5km, turning off at the junction marked N-636, direction Elorrio. Continue towards Elorrio, passing a commercial centre, a roundabout, a railway crossing, and two further roundabouts. Once you've passed through Abadino, Look out for a sign on the right marked Atxondo and Axpe. Take this road through Apatamonasterio and after 1km, there will be a turning for Axpe on your right. The villlage is 1km later down this road and the restaurant is located on the main square (Plaza St Juan), opposite the church.

Arguinzoniz has a different charcoal for each ingredient he cooks

sturdy cuts of meat like beef, and subtle applewood for more pronounced tastes like oysters and caviar.

And he's created his own grill on which to cook them: six custom-made grills that are moved up and down during cooking through an ingenious system of tracks and pulleys, his raw produce placed in small baskets at varying levels about the charcoal. Each ingredient demands its own precise timing and heat intensity, he says, including ingredients that you just wouldn't expect to be grilled, like eggs and caviar. All this in a simple farmhouse in the tiny Basque village of Axpe, 45 minutes south east of Bilbao.

But, of course, the Basque country is known for its asadors (grill houses) and it was this heritage that inspired Arguinzoniz to buy a half-ruined restaurant in a 200-year-old building on the main square. He didn't want this tradition to be lost: 'The aroma of wood smoke became etched in my memory when I was a child,' he says. 'The houses in our village had no electricity or heating other than the traditional hearth, where women simmered beans and stews for hours.'

While it still embodies all the essence of a traditional asador, the turning point for Etxebarri came about ten years ago as a result of Arguinzoniz's desire to expand the repertoire of the grill and its ability to enhance a wide variety of produce, whether it be the cooking of risotto in a saucepan with laser-drilled fine holes, the delicate sautéing of baby eels, or the grilling of caviar.

So advanced now is his ability to smoke and grill that Arguinzoniz uses no sauces to enhance his flavours. Food is simply presented: grilled prawns in their shell; ember-warmed oysters with fresh wakame, or baby octopus lightly chargrilled and served with its own ink. And most of his ingredients come from the kitchen garden or surrounding area. The restaurant even makes its own Iberico pork chorizo sausage.

ON ORDER

Plaza San Juan 1, 48291 Axpe-Marzana, Atxondo-Bizkaia, Spain

+34 94 658 3042; www.asadoretxebarri.com

Head chef: *Victor Arguinzoniz*

On the menu: *The best produce available on the day*

Did you know? *Arguinzoniz produces a smoked ice-cream by heating the milk over coals*

Top tip: *Sample at least one of the products made in-house, including cured chorizo, hand-pressed cheeses, black pudding, ice-creams and smoked wild salmon*

Approximate cost for two: *€240, not including wine*

LES AMBASSADEURS

It would have to be a very hard-hearted and jaded traveller who can stand and look outside the door of the Hôtel de Crillon without feeling at least slightly moved. Ahead, the traffic rushes seemingly at random across the wide Place de la Concorde (there are no unsightly road markings to sully the immaculate cobbles) and it's impossible to turn one's head without catching sight of yet another iconic landmark. Oh, look, it's the Eiffel Tower, the Louvre, Les Invalides… The whole of Paris is out there in its gilded splendour, and one could poke one's head out of the door here and feel one had truly 'done' Paris. Which would leave plenty of time to step back inside for a taste of one of the grandest and most ambitious dining rooms in the city – Les Ambassadeurs.

The restaurant is located in the ballroom of this former private house, which was commissioned in 1758 by Louis XV, but then acquired by the Comte de Crillon in 1788. It remained in the Crillon family until it was transformed into a hotel, which opened in 1909.

Inventing food

One of his Piège's amuse-bouches is his platter of 'TV snacks' which plays on the kind of tray you might take to the sofa with a soda and some pizza on it – except in this case the soda is an intriguing glass of carbonated carrot or beetroot juice and the pizza comes in the form of a crisp croquette that yields in the mouth to liquefied essence of pizza. He has also revisited some classic dishes such as oeufs en cocotte, which he makes by placing a whole egg yolk within an emulsion of egg white, studded with chive and truffle, and cooking it in the oven to serve with chive oil and truffle. 'It's a very fine, light dish,' he says.

'Cooking exists at a particular time for a given society. We didn't eat the same way 10 years ago and we won't eat the same way in 10 years time'

The room is as lavish and unrestrained as one would hope with such a setting. There are marble floors, marble walls edged with gold, friezes, chandeliers, mirrors set into high, arched recesses to reflect and echo the light coming in through identically shaped windows swagged with opulent fabrics to fall upon extravagantly laid tables and elegantly attired staff.

The chef here is Jean-François Piège, the former protégé of Alain Ducasse, whose restaurant at the Plaza Athénée he used to head. Growing up near Valence in south east France, though, Piège had always wanted to be a gardener rather than a cook until, he says, 'Gradually my passion for planting and harvesting products transformed into a passion for the products themselves and finally for cooking.'

Piège describes his food as being part of a 'traditional yet permissive' movement. 'Cooking exists at a particular time for a given society. We didn't eat the same way 10 years ago and we won't eat the same way in 10 years time.' It doesn't come as a surprise that Piège's food is playful, and given his horticultural instincts, that his ingredients are impeccably sourced.

He won't speak about 'creating' dishes; for him it's a matter of 'composing' dishes according to techniques and seasonal ingredients. 'The menu is short, so we change things all the time,' he says – indeed, some items on the menu are tagged with a date to distinguish them from previous interpretations of the same dish. But the foundation of Piège's cuisine is traditional: 'Cuisine starts with the best produce,' he says. Which for him means, for example, Galician beef and langoustines from Scotland. In the end, he insists that it's not whether his cooking is modern, molecular or anything except pleasing the customer. 'It's just a question of being good and making people happy.'

ON ORDER

Hôtel Le Crillon, 10 Place de la Concorde, 75008 Paris, France

+33 (0)1 4471 1616; www.crillon.com

Head chef: *Jean-François Piège*

On the menu: *Langoustines, sushi, golden Iranian caviar*

Watch out for: *Piège's inventive amuse-bouches (see opposite page)*

Top tip: *Guests can assemble their own tasting menus by choosing three dishes from the à la carte menu, which are served in half portions along with cheese and desserts for €210*

Approximate cost for two: *The four-course lunch menu costs €156 for two, not including service or wine. Expect to pay in the region of €400 for a three-course dinner with wine*

L'ARPÈGE

Born in Brittany in 1956 to a father who was a musician and a mother who was a dressmaker, Alain Passard learned early in life the importance of a deft touch. But it was his grandmother Louise who first instilled in him his love of cooking. She shared with him the excitement of shopping for and preparing a meal for others, and also her skill and enthusiasm for cooking using flame – from roasting to rotisserie. In spite of that, he admits that cooking was just one of several paths he could have chosen. 'Manual work was very important to my family,' he says, 'but I suppose it was easier to be a restaurant chef than anything else, because there were lots of good restaurants around.' Had he not become a chef, however, he says he would probably have been a musician, and the name of his restaurant, which means 'arpeggio' (or 'broken chord') references his continuing love of music, as well as being an invitation for the diner to find similarities between the beauty and harmonies of music, and those of a wonderful meal.

Apprenticed at 15 to a restaurant in Brittany, Passard continued to learn the classical techniques at La Chaumière in Reims, under chef Gaston Boyer,

The raw ingredient

Alain Passard made headlines in 2001 when he announced that red meat was off the menu and instead, vegetables would be centre stage. 'There are restaurants specialising in meat and fish,' he said at the time. 'So why not vegetables?' He did not turn his restaurant vegetarian, as was widely reported. Rather than turning away from meat he was turning towards vegetables, which he felt offered a better canvas for the subtle interplay of 'gesture' on behalf of the chef, and raw ingredient. 'For me, I think the great dishes of the future will be ones that are hardly touched by the cook,' he has said. 'Perhaps there will be a single gesture, but it will be one of such precision that it will encapsulate 15 or so movements.'

This kind of approach demands the best ingredients, and the majority come from the restaurant's own organic gardens in the Sarthe, near Le Mans, 220km from Paris. Produce is harvested in the early morning – at the height of summer some 800kg per month – and put on the train to arrive at the restaurant in time for lunch. The waste from the kitchen makes the return journey to be composted. All of which makes the restaurant an environmentalist's dream. Instead of using chemicals, the gardeners have a lake for frogs to keep down slugs, and keep bees to insure pollination and provide honey for the restaurant's desserts.

'There are no noble products. Only good and bad products'

before moving to Paris to work with Alain Senderens at L'Archestrate. His first solo venture was the Duc d'Enghien at the Casino d'Enghien, followed by a stint at Le Cariton in Brussels. He finally opened L'Arpège in October 1986 on the site formerly occupied by L'Archestrate, the very restaurant in which he'd worked with Senderens.

The restaurant's design references the 1930s, with a sensuously curved wooden wall that wraps itself around the restaurant, punctuated by Lalique glass panels which are echoed by the plates on the tables. The look is in complete contrast with many other Paris restaurants at this level – not for him the heavy curtains and elaborate table settings. In fact, here the windows themselves are the focal point, made in unique wave-patterned glass by Bernard Pictet. There's just one picture on the wall, that of his grandmother Louise Passard, who started him on the journey to becoming a chef.

Simplicity of décor is matched by the purity of flavours on the plate. Passard does not hold with the idea that there exists a hierarchy of ingredients, with some exalted foodstuffs (lobsters, truffles, foie gras) held in higher esteem than others. 'There are no noble products,' he insists. 'Only good and bad products.' So you can expect otherwise humble ingredients to be given the five-star treatment here. For example, Passard will take a beetroot and bake it in salt, then 'carve' it tableside – a level of ceremony one isn't accustomed to seeing in the context of a root vegetable – before serving it with 25-year-old balsamic vinegar. Other dishes include gazpacho of tomato with mustard ice-cream (Passard experiments continually with tomato varieties, so expect this dish to taste different from one visit to the next) and an ever-changing variant on the theme of fresh ravioli in broth.

ON ORDER

84 Rue de Varenne, 75007 Paris, France

+33 (0)1 4705 0906; www.alain-passard.com

Head chef: *Alain Passard*

On the menu: *Ravioli in seasonal vegetable broth*

Watch out for: *Alain Passard often comes into the dining room to have a bite to eat near the end of the service*

Top tip: *Don't forget your wallet, this is rumoured to be one of the most expensive dining experiences in Paris*

Approximate cost for two: *The tasting menu is €360 per person. Wine starts at €70 a bottle*

TANTRIS

The restaurant that is said to have heralded the start of a new era in German gastronomy, Tantris is the brainchild of Munich property developer Fritz Eichbauer and chef Eckart Witzigmann. They wanted to apply the basic principles of tantric philosophy to cuisine with the aim of 'finding a balance between the body and mind; not asceticism but pleasure without remorse'. The result is a unique combination of 1970s architecture with Oriental-style sculptures and a cuisine that both challenges and inspires.

The manifestation of an 'attitude to life' and with a philosophy that food is the basis for happiness, Tantris – two-Michelin-starred – took five years to make its mark. 'We practically had to educate our guests', Eichbauer has said. 'Back then [in 1971] there was nothing in Germany similar to what we were doing, and definitely not in Munich.'

The restaurant's location is the first surprise (hidden in the drab, concrete landscape of the Schwabing Business Park), quickly followed by its décor – a modern, bright, poppy venue with primary colours on its walls and on its plates, the orange carpet stretching from floor to ceiling, plastic orange

A 1970s flashback

'Exotic' and 'strange' is how Justus Dahinden, a Zurich architect, described the intention behind the restaurant he built in 1971. Since then its 1970s pop look has been renovated and updated (slightly) by Stefan Braunfels in 2002. The exposed concrete remains, but the carpets that reach between the floors and the ceilings have been refreshed and lightened via a wall of mirrors and a radiant use of light. He also got rid of the pink tables, now a more complimentary and sensible brown. The garden space has also been reopened, allowing guests use of a sculpture-packed nod to the East.

'We practically had to educate our guests – back then there was nothing in Germany similar to what we were doing'

lampshades hanging over each table, and bright orange and red artwork decorating the walls. The orange, red and black of the setting is frequently reflected on the dining plates: in lobster terrines, truffle salads, sepia risotto and tomato coulis.

Original chef Witzigmann was followed by Heinz Winkler (a then unknown chef from Austria who won the restaurant three Michelin stars) and, since 1991, Hans Haas, who has made his mark here with his personal take on high-class cookery. He won *Gault Millau*'s chef of the year in 1995 and has his own cookery school that he opened in 2005.

Under his direction, the cuisine at Tantris is subtle but adventurous, offered via an eight-course menu that changes daily, plus a set five-course menu, that comes with wine, as well as a more traditional à la carte offering. The more informal Tantris-Lounge offers an intriguing 'finger food' variation of the main restaurant's cuisine.

Tantris is all about the guests, says Haas. 'We only have one desire: to offer them a culinary experience that they've never had before.' This Tantris does through its seasonal menus that can include anything from oxtail broth to venison cutlet with green asparagus, risotto, Périgord truffle cream and schupfnudein (potato noodles); and spinny lobster on pea purée and lime-ginger sauce.

Haas's dishes are complemented by the expertise of sommelier Paula Bosch, who has been at Tantris since 1991. 'It is about each guest and their palate,' she says. 'I endeavour to discern their preferences, so that I can select the best wine for them from our cellar of over 70,000 bottles.' For Bosch, it's about opening up a new dimension of wine to each individual guest, delighting them with new flavours that enhance the qualities of each dish.

ON ORDER

Johann-Fichte-Strasse 7, 80805 Munich, Germany

+49 (0)893 619590; www.tantris.de

Head chef: *Hans Haas*

On the menu: *Haas changes the menu twice daily, but expect to find dishes such as suckling pig with smoked eel and dried plums or lukewarm seppioline filled with egg yolk served with sauce mignonette*

Did you know? *Haas has his own cooking school. You can experience his attitude towards food and preparation under the chef himself by booking via www.hans-haas.de*

Top tip: *Book into Tantris-Lounge – this exclusive restaurant serves Michelin-prized 'finger food'*

Approximate cost for two: *There are various arrangements. For example, a five-course menu including wines costs €300 for two on Tuesdays, Wednesdays and Thursdays*

OAXEN SKÄRGÅRDSKROG

'We might call ourselves a restaurant of the archipelago', says head chef and proprietor Magnus Ek, 'but that doesn't mean that the cuisine we produce is simple or stuck in the past.' In fact, Oaxen Skärgårdskrog is anything but. Ek's experimental and sustainable approach to Swedish gastronomy makes the restaurant well worth the hour-long trip from Stockholm.

Located on Oaxen, a small island in the Stockholm archipelago, the restaurant can only be reached via boat from Mörkö. It is run by Ek and his partner (and sommelier) Agneta Green in an old quarry manager's house in Himmerfjärden Bay, which is overlooked by woods packed with the white truffles of which Ek is so fond. Here, Ek conjures up his four menus: à la carte, five-course, vegetarian and tasting, all with dishes that reflect Ek's adventurous approach to local ingredients – for example, uniting duck liver with cardamom sugar and juniper, or baking halibut in burnt grass.

Take away at Pumpen

If you can't reserve a table at Oaxen Skärgårdskrog and you arrive by private boat, you can always eat at Magnus Ek and Agnetha Green's smaller and more informal venue, the open-air cafe Pumpen. It serves a variety of simple, tasty fare, such as smoked shrimps, fish casserole, herring and homemade grilled sausages, with the option to eat beside the pier or take away on to your own boat.

'The dishes reflect Ek's adventurous approach to local ingredients'

'We have woken up from a French dream,' Ek says. 'It used to be easier to use imported products.' Now he opts instead for local seafood, berries and even dried roseroot (*Rhodiola rosea*) and birch sap, as well as the age-old Swedish food-preserving techniques like salting, pickling and smoking fish. Think pickled herring, but updated and more delicate.

All of Ek's classic dishes are here: smoked warm Norwegian lobster with cream cheese and purée of confited cabbage; or Swedish duck liver with white beans in caramel; and veal brawn with hazelnut bread, asparagus and champagne cream. But his tasting menu is at times even more unusual and challenging, such as in his confited pig's head and black pudding bread served with glazed Jerusalem artichoke and marmalade of apples, or his egg of isomalt with truffle cream on crumble from crispy oven pancake served with caviar in jelly of distilled rockweed and pâté of rabbit.

Even his desserts are experimental and grandiose, such as his goat's milk cheesecake in burnt bay leaves, chèvre from Ljusterö and foam of 'Karl Johan' served with garden cress purée, macadamia nut and crispy rockweed, or his sea buckthorn chocolate sorbet with ice-smoked lemon verbena and shortcrust pastry, served with strawberries in distilled sea buckthorn juice.

It's an avant-garde dream that belies the restaurant's location in an isolated mansion that seats only 40 guests at a time. Those who can't tear themselves away when the last boat departs the island can reserve a cabin on the restaurant's 19th-century steamship, *m/s Florence*, tethered to the dock (30 April to 31 October only). With its luxury oak, ebony, Brazilian rosewood and marble décor, it provides the perfect accompaniment to both the cuisine and the beauty of the archipelago night.

ON ORDER

SE-153 93 Mörkö, Sweden

+46 (0)8 5515 3105; www.oaxenkrog.se

Head chef-owner: *Magnus Ek*

On the menu: *Scallop and Swedish cuttlefish with purée of leek, foamy juice from fennel and 'forgotten' fishparts*

Did you know? *Oaxen Skärgårdskrog was voted Ecological Restaurant of the Year in 2007 for its ability to 'bring out great characters of taste from ecological products and local raw materials'*

Top tip: *You can only arrive at Oaxen on the daily ferry (departing twice an hour from Mörkö, last ferry back from Oaxen 10.30pm Sunday to Friday and 12.30am on Saturday). Most guests book into the boat-hotel m/s Florence for the night*

Approximate cost for two: *The three-course menu costs 1,700 kr for two, wine starts at 535 kr a bottle*

ROCKPOOL
(FISH)

An almost-newcomer to the list. Trish Richards and Neil Perry's Rockpool (fish) is the latest incarnation of the Rockpool restaurant. Confusingly, it stands on exactly the same spot – and is, more often than not, referred to as Rockpool, without the (fish) tag – but the change is nonetheless distinctive and engaging.

The difference is in the approach: Neil Perry recently turned 50 and is experiencing a newly refreshed, almost playful attitude to his food. After 19 years striving for perfection in haute cuisine, he closed the previous Rockpool on 20 October 2007 and reopened it 12 days later as a more casual seafood venue. Tasting menus have gone, and in their place came bare tables, à la carte dishes, a relaxed attitude to dining and some simple international cooking that showcases the quality of the seafood available off the Sydney coast. And what quality there is.

'The cornerstone of good cooking is to source the finest produce,' says Perry. 'We wanted to make Rockpool (fish) more accessible and have

From the kitchen
Korean-style tuna tartare (serves 4 as a starter)

Ingredients:

2 medium carrots

4 spring onions

400g piece yellowfin tuna

1 small Chinese cabbage heart, finely shredded

Leaves from 1 bunch coriander

3 tablespoons roasted pine nuts

Sesame dressing

4 egg yolks

2 tablespoons sesame seeds, toasted

Freshly ground white pepper

Method:

Cut the carrot and spring onions into a fine julienne and soak in ice water for half an hour. Place the tuna on a chopping board, and remove the skin. Cut it into rounds of ½cm thickness, then cut it lengthwise into strips of about ½cm square. Place the tuna, carrots, spring onions, cabbage, coriander, pine nuts and dressing in a bowl. Toss in sesame dressing and divide between four plates. Make a little well in the centre of each and place an egg yolk on top. Sprinkle with sesame seeds and grind over some pepper. Serve immediately.

'We wanted it to have something for everyone, whether it's a simple dish or an amazing piece of fish cooked with more complexity'

the customer in complete control of their dining experience, so we created a menu which allowed them to design their own meal, by choosing from a large variety of seafood. We wanted it to have something for everyone, whether it's a simple dish or an amazing piece of fish cooked with more complexity.' Now diners can choose from as many as 10 different preparations for each of the entrées, salads and sides as well as fish, shellfish and non-seafood main plates. There's even a gourmet Moroccan-style fish burger that comes with a more-than-reasonable price tag of AUS$14, given the high quality of the ingredients and the cuisine.

The mood is smart-casual, only 'no shorts, singlets, or thongs please'. The daily-changing menu runs from Japanese-inspired sashimi to Mediterranean salads, pasta and grills, as well as old Rockpool classics, live shellfish and whole fish to share. Its commitment to sourcing ethically has remained constant.

'Sustainable fishing is important to us and we want customers to know that when they dine at Rockpool (fish) our fishermen fish sustainably and catch using a minimal stress regime,' says Perry. 'We also make sure our shellfish are kept alive and stress-free, and we dry fillet to maintain quality and we cook with care.

'We need to value our seafood resource in this country for it to last future generations. Too much is mistreated and undervalued, and as a result, taste and texture is compromised,' he explains. 'Fishermen must be rewarded for their efforts. We could buy cheap, inferior fish, but this would compromise our philosophy in delivering the best.'

And it is the best that they do deliver, including signature dishes such as tuna sashimi salad; king prawns with goat's cheese tortellini and burnt butter; stir-fried spanner crab omelette and a variety of whole and dry filleted fish and live shellfish that can be plain grilled, breaded, pan roasted, steamed and more.

ON ORDER

107 George Street, The Rocks, Sydney, NSW 2000, Australia

+61 (0)2 9252 1888; www.rockpoolsydney.com

Head chef-owner: *Neil Perry and executive chef Michael McEnearney*

On the menu: *Hand-picked crystal crab, avocado, chickpea and roast pepper salad with pomegranate*

Did you know? *One of the menu's oldest dishes, the stir-fried crab omelette, was on the original menu in 1992 – and was back on for the reopening of Rockpool (fish)*

Top tip: *Ask for recommendations on the wine menu – it includes an impressive selection of over 850 wines from Australia and around the world*

Approximate cost for two: *A three-course meal will cost around AUS$300 for two, including wine, but you can also order light but equally tasty bar snacks from AUS$14*

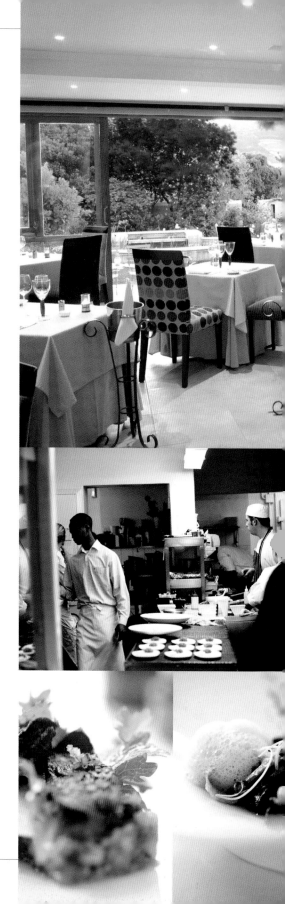

LE QUARTIER FRANÇAIS

An exclusive boutique hotel tucked away in the heart of the Franschhoek Valley, in the Cape Winelands in South Africa, Le Quartier Français is actually the name of the hotel, rather than the restaurant (of which there are three). Traditionally, visitors have come to Le Quartier Français to explore the surrounding Franschhoek Mountains and the Western Cape, but increasingly it has been the cutting-edge cuisine of Margot Janse and her team at The Tasting Room that has been drawing the crowds, and that isn't likely to change any time soon.

This is South African cooking at its most adventurous. Margot Janse is constantly evolving culinary creations like foie gras and sultana mousse with pain d'épice and rhubarb and beetroot jelly, and Norwegian salmon terrine with fennel marmalade. For Margot the secret lies in her boundless love for what she does. 'It is not about achievements, but the joy of making a living by doing what I love best. My work allows me to express myself and offers the best of all – to be appreciated.' But she's equally grateful to the local ingredients: 'Franschhoek has amazing produce.

I love it when women from the village arrive on my doorstep with black figs, berries or nettles. My food style is about being creative. Certain things are logical. Before starting anything you must know what you want to achieve. This applies to food as well. I know in my head what a dish will taste like.'

Signature dishes, such as pepper-crusted Franschhoek salmon trout with seaweed, ossobucco and periwinkle, and tuna tartare 'cannelloni' delight the senses. Guests can choose a four-, six- or eight-course menu, which also includes plenty of playful desserts, such as coconut parfait, sable and roasted pineapple crème brûlée.

ON ORDER

16 Huguenot Road, Franschhoek, 7690, Western Cape, South Africa

+27 (0)21 876 2151; www.lequartier.co.za

Executive chef: *Margot Janse*

On the menu: *Kudu and biltong consommé, chilled gem squash and buchu foam*

Did you know? *Le Quartier Français is also an exclusive boutique hotel. You can book accommodation here in one of its Four Quarters Suites, Auberge Suites or in one of 15 luxury rooms located around a central swimming pool*

Top tip: *The serious fine dining takes place in The Tasting Room, but for a more relaxed atmosphere, you can also book into iCi, a cafe-style bistro bar with a street-side terrace*

Approximate cost for two: *The eight-course menu costs R2,160 for two, including a wine pairing with each course*

THE
S.PELLEGRINO
WORLD'S
50
BEST
RESTAURANTS
POSITIONS 51 TO 100

51 TAILLEVENT
Paris, France
Web: www.taillevent.com

Established in 1946 in a grand 19th-century townhouse just off the Champs-Elysées, Taillevent is one of the finest dining institutions in Paris. Under the control of head chef Alain Solivérès since 2002 (formerly head chef at Elysées du Vernet, where he earned two Michelin stars), the restaurant's culinary philosophy is 'haute cuisine based on simplicity', which is reflected in its ever-changing menu. Dishes range from duck liver accompanied by spice bread and ginger; cassoulet of crayfish and Scottish salmon with an olive oil and lemon sauce. The wine list is reputed to be among the best in Paris, with over 2,400 varieties on offer.

52 NOBU
New York, USA
Web: www.noburestaurants.com

One of Japan's most famous exports, Nobu Matsuhisa has been wowing the West with his creative take on modern Japanese cuisine since he opened his first Nobu restaurant in New York in 1994. Launched in association with one of America's most respected and celebrated restaurateurs, Drew Nieporent, and Oscar-winning actor Robert de Niro, Nobu's menu showcases the results of a hard-earned classical training in Tokyo sushi bars with the influence of culinary experiences learnt in Peru and Argentina. The resulting dishes, such as 'new-style' sashimi; lobster with wasabi pepper sauce; and buttery textured broiled black cod marinated with miso, sake, mirin and sugar, have established Nobu New York at the cutting edge of Japanese food.

53 OSTERIA FRANCESCANA
Modena, Italy
Web: www.osteriafrancescana.it

Traditional flavours and entrepreneurial spirit are combined at Osteria Francescana, so it was little surprise when the restaurant earned its second Michelin star in 2005. Hidden away in the winding streets of ancient Modena, it's not the easiest venue to find, but if you persist you'll be well rewarded by head chef Massimo Batturo's innovative menu. A former protégé of Alain Ducasse, Batturo is known for his impressive variations on langoustine risotto, foie gras terrine and suckling pig, not to mention a signature dish blending five different ages of Parmesan cheese. Don't miss one of his famed reinterpretations of classic puddings, such as zuppa Inglese, a dark chocolate pudding set on strips of cake and served with ginger-vanilla ice-cream and jellied slices of the red Tuscan liqueur Alkermes.

54 MASA
New York, USA
Web: www.masanyc.com

Two keywords define the Masa style of cooking: 'shibui', simplicity devoid of unnecessary elements and the honest presentation of materials; and 'umami', what the Japanese term the basic essence or flavour inherent in each ingredient. This measured approach to cuisine is also reflected in the décor: Masa's eponymous restaurant purposefully transports diners out of New York's neon-draped city streets into the seclusion of a 26-seat sushi temple, replete with bamboo garden. Meals begin with five carefully composed appetisers, followed by a sushi entrée of 15 to 20 kinds of seafood flown in directly from Japan.

55 BUKHARA
New Delhi, India
Web: www.itcwelcomgroup.in

Bukhara's menu hasn't changed since it opened in 1973, which is not to say that its dishes aren't innovative or surprising. Following in the footsteps of the late Mandanlal Jaiswal, current head chef JP Singh has chosen to focus on tradition. It has proved a formula for success, attracting the likes of Bill Clinton and Vladimir Putin to Bukhara's tables in recent years. The venue was also rewarded with the Best Restaurant in Asia Award at the 2008 S.Pellegrino World's 50 Best Restaurants event. Veterans advise that the best way to experience Bukhara's variety is to order an assorted kebab platter, followed by its classic lamb (raan) dishes, accompanied by a thin butter naan. If that isn't enough to fill you up, finish off with a traditional rice-based phirni pudding or one of Bukhara's amazing ice-cream kulfis.

L'Atelier de Joël Robuchon
London, UK

56 L'AMBROISIE
Paris, France
Web: www.ambroisie-placedesvosges.com

A 17th-century townhouse decorated in the style of an Italian palazzo but located in the heart of Paris, L'Ambroisie is nothing short of grand. Fortunately, the food more than lives up to the décor under the measured skill of head chef Bernard Pacaud, whose approach to classic French cuisine brought the restaurant three Michelin stars and widespread critical acclaim. Dishes change seasonally and could include anything from flash-cooked sea bass layered with goose liver, truffles and rosemary-scented artichokes to fricassée of Breton lobster with chestnuts, served with purée of pumpkin. The cellar is equally faultless, run by exemplary sommelier Pierre Le Moullac.

57 MAZE
London, UK
Web: www.gordonramsay.com/maze

Based in London's dignified Grosvenor Square, Maze is one of celebrity chef Gordon Ramsay's key UK businesses. It is run by executive chef Jason Atherton, who cut his teeth at Verre in Dubai, where he learned under the watchful eyes of Pierre Koffman, Nico Ladenis and Gordon Ramsay himself. Maze sees him take centre stage with a daily changing menu of market specials, comprising six starters, plus main course and desserts. And if that all sounds too much, there's also a wide variety of tasting dishes, many of which are cooked on a charcoal robata grill, in the wood oven or on the plancha.

58 THE RIVER CAFÉ
London, UK
Web: www.rivercafe.co.uk

A little taste of Italy in the heart of London, The River Café was opened by Rose Gray and Ruth Rogers in 1987 in order to recreate the flavours of traditional Italian home cooking in a modern setting. Accompanied by an all-Italian wine list and a relaxing, open dining atmosphere, Gray and Rogers' menu is a seasonal feast that draws on the very best of Italy's culinary heritage.

Expect to see delicacies such as insalata di Dicembre with roasted pheasant, Parma ham, chestnuts, trevise, pomegranate and aged balsamic vinegar.

59 STEIRERECK
Vienna, Austria
Web: www.steirereck.at

Widely considered to be Austria's leading restaurant, Steirereck occupies an atmospheric pavilion that overlooks the Stadtpark, one of the country's most beautiful locations. As its setting may suggest, Steirereck is elegant and formal, which isn't to say that it takes itself too seriously. Head chef Heinz Reitbauer's family has been running this place since 1970 and they've made it into a characterful and welcoming venue that offers its own unique line of innovative Austrian cuisine. Outstanding fish dishes are followed by a choice of 120 cheeses from 13 countries, all stored in Steirereck's own cellar.

60 LE CHÂTEAUBRIAND
Paris, France
Phone: +33 (0)1 4357 4595

This year's 'Breakthrough Restaurant', Le Châteaubriand is the one to watch in the next 12 months. In order to be put forward for this award, the restaurant must be under five years old, have not appeared in the top 50 list previously and must be emerging as the latest 'hot property'. Le Châteaubriand meets these criteria and more; it has been described as the leader of the so-called 'bistronomy' movement, bringing haute cuisine to customers at affordable prices in a bistro setting. To do this, chef Inaki Aizpitarte combines Asian, Central American, Israeli and Egyptian influences to create exciting fusion dishes, such as poached foie gras with poppy seeds and red cabbage gazpacho.

61 OBAUER
Werfen, Austria
Web: www.obauer.com

Brothers Karl and Rudi Obauer have been running restaurant Obauer since 1979, drawing upon extensive experience picked up while working in restaurants together all over Austria and abroad. Much of their knowledge of upmarket classic and creative cuisine was developed when training under Alain Chapel, Emile Jung and the Troisgros brothers. The resulting dishes are as gorgeous to behold as they are to eat, with main courses including lamb with herb salad, and catfish with tomatoes and capers. A beautiful raspberry soufflé offers a palette-cleansing choice for dessert. The setting is equally compelling; part of *The Sound of Music* was filmed on the outskirts of the village of Werfen.

62 DIETER MÜLLER
Lerbacher Weg, *Germany*
Web: *www.dietermueller.de*

Situated in a luxurious country pile in Germany's Bergisches Land, Dieter Müller's restaurant promises refined, classical cooking. The cuisine is a fusion of classic French, Mediterranean and Asian influences, creating a varied and interesting menu. Highlights include the gratinated saddle of Müritz lamb with a jus of chorizo, slices of grilled vegetables and lamb's sweetbreads, and the mildly smoked etouffé pigeon on a compote of beetroot, jus of aniseed and pepper, baby corn and a crisp tartar of pigeon. Desserts are equally daring in their combinations, such as marinated pineapple with leaves of brittle, and guacamole tarragon sorbet with banana espuma.

63 WD-50
New York, *USA*
Web: *www.wd-50.com*

Since opening WD-50 in 2003, Wylie Dufresne has worked hard to establish his name on the New York restaurant scene. 'Avant-garde cuisine' or 'molecular gastronomy' are labels often applied to his style of cooking, and his passion for daring combinations and experimentation make for an unusual menu. A three-course meal might feature, for example, popcorn soup, followed by roasted wagyu flat-iron steak paired with coffee-flavoured gnocchi and a gel of coconut milk. To finish, a dessert of white chocolate with white beer ice-cream. Dining at WD-50 is not for the fainthearted, but for those with a taste for adventure it is well worth the visit.

64 ZUMA
London, *UK*
Web: *www.zumarestaurant.com*

Zuma, in London's upmarket Knightsbridge, is the epitome of a great, modern Japanese restaurant. From its minimalist interior to its sophisticated cuisine, it is precision and poise encapsulated, but it's also a lot of fun. Chef and owner Rainer Becker has developed an innovative style of dining with five cleverly apportioned spaces for eating or drinking: the main dining area, the chef's table, kotatsu room, sushi counter and robata grill. Highlights include thinly sliced sea bass with yuzu, truffle oil and salmon roe; and crispy fried squid with green chilli salt.

65 LA PERGOLA
Rome, *Italy*
Web: *www.heinzbeck.com*

He's German and cooks in an American hotel, yet Heinz Beck is one of Rome's best-loved chefs. That's less surprising when you taste the unique twist on Italian haute cuisine that he has been delighting critics and diners with at La Pergola since 1994. Known for its balance, harmony and unusual flavour combinations, highlights from Beck's menu include pasta tagliolini with shrimp, fresh lime and zucchini flowers, and pigeon and duck liver with a mustard-seed sauce. The rooftop location at the Cavalieri Hilton hotel provides a spectacular view over Rome's skyline.

66 EL POBLET
Alicante, *Spain*
Web: *www.elpoblet.com*

One of Europe's most avant-garde restaurants, El Poblet draws its vast aesthetic inspiration from the mind of head chef Quique Dacosta. Not content to serve mere food, Dacosta instead prefers his dishes to represent whole environments – so a seaweed and mushroom salad will take diners on a beachfront stroll, while oysters cooked until their shells explode will convey a similar experience to viewing abstract architecture. The abstraction continues into the kitchen, bar and wine cellar, which all open to each other inside a glass shell.

67 THE SQUARE
London, UK
Web: www.squarerestaurant.org

Notching up two Michelin stars and four AA rosettes in 2007, The Square is emerging as a force to be reckoned with in London's competitive restaurant scene. Owned by Nigel Platts-Martin and chef Philip Howard, the kitchen blends Howard's talents with those of Robert Weston – plus impeccable seasonal ingredients. Lunches can include, among others, velouté of cauliflower with truffle Chantilly. One eye-catching dish on the à la carte menu is lasagne of Dorset crab with cappuccino of shellfish and a champagne foam.

68 RESIDENZ HEINZ WINKLER
Aschau im Chiemgau, Germany
Web: www.residenz-heinz-winkler.de

If there were a chefs' hall of fame, Heinz Winkler's name would definitely be up there. In 1981, Winkler was the youngest chef to receive three Michelin stars while at Tantris in Munich (see page 182). He established his own gastronomic hot spot in the Bavarian countryside in 1991. Situated in a 600-year-old coaching inn, Residenz Heinz Winkler combines classical French principles with the Bavarian flourishes for which Winkler has become world famous. Seventeen years on, Winkler is still going strong and shows no signs of slowing up.

69 48, THE RESTAURANT
Athens, Greece
Web: www.48therestaurant.com

Best known for his partnership with Joël Robuchon, businessman Theodore Margellos is also the business force behind 48 in Athens. As a concept, 48 shares similar principles to the Robuchon enterprise, combining the virtues of a fashionable bar with outstanding food and wine at reasonable prices, but this time it is head chef Christoforos Peskias behind the stove. Known for his light-hearted combination of traditional Greek styles with international flavours, Peskias's menu changes according to the chef's creative spirit and availability of seasonal ingredients.

70 THE WATERSIDE INN
Bray, UK
Web: www.waterside-inn.co.uk

They may be best known for opening La Gavroche (see page 98), but the Roux brothers have also put the tiny town of Bray on the culinary map. Opened in 1972, The Waterside Inn was awarded its first Michelin star two years later, and by 1985 it had received all three, which it has retained ever since. Unashamedly French in approach, the Waterside's menu is a seasonal delight that offers anything from roasted Challandais duck with lightly spiced prunes, green puy lentils and a Grande Chartreuse jus to pan-fried lobster medallion with a white port sauce and ginger vegetable julienne.

71 L'AUBERGE DU PONT DE COLLONGES
Lyon, France
Web: www.bocuse.fr

Chef-proprietor Paul Bocuse is undoubtedly one of the 20th-century's finest chefs, which is not to say that he isn't still a major force in the 21st. Located just north of Lyon, L'Auberge du Pont de Collonges can be found in Collonges-au-Mont-d'Or, the village where Bocuse himself was born and raised. He draws on the best of the area's local produce – from starters like scallop of foie gras, pan-cooked and served with verjus and lightly browned potatoes, and casseroled Burgundy snails with traditional parsley butter, to main courses that include sea bass stuffed with lobster mousse in a puff-pastry shell.

72 ESPERANTO
Stockholm, Sweden
Web: www.esperantorestaurant.se

A little-known Swedish restaurant with a bright future, Esperanto is another establishment to watch. Combining experimental cookery with nutritional flair, the restaurant offers a selection of innovative and healthy dishes inspired by the cuisines of North Africa, southern Europe and Japan. The menu features everything from frozen cream of fresh garlic in boneflour and celery salt to salt-poached suckling lamb with white onion butter and spring vegetables. Candied rose petals make for an unusual dessert.

73 L'ARNSBOURG
Baerenthal, near Strasbourg, France
Web: www.arnsbourg.com

Hidden in the Vosgnes mountains of Alsace-Lorraine, L'Arnsbourg is one of France's most remote culinary destinations. But with guests travelling here from as far away as Japan, it is also one of France's most frequented and highly regarded, thanks to three-star Michelin chef Jean-Georges Klein's bold use of flavour combinations. Klein's creations are best sampled in one of his degustation menus (look out for his signature dish of potato purée with truffle mousse, prepared to look like a cappuccino).

74 AKELARRE
San Sebastián, Spain
Web: www.akelarre.net

Overlooking the Bay of Biscay, Basque chef Pedro Subijana couldn't have chosen a more attractive setting for his restaurant when he opened it in 1974. But despite the farmhouse exterior, Akelarre is a modern kitchen producing innovative and often daring interpretations of local seafood dishes, such as his hake fillets in sauce with kokotxas (the hake jaw). He also draws on plenty of inland specialities, such as his foie gras on spongy 'talo', Txakoli caramel and vinegar caviar. The dessert selection promises more amazing combinations such as his infamous gin-tonic on a plate.

75 SANT PAU
Sant Pol de Mar, near Barcelona, Spain
Web: www.ruscalleda.com

About an hour's train ride from central Barcelona, Sant Pau is more than worth the journey. Located in the picturesque seaside town of Sant Pol de Mar, this is where you'll get to sample the cooking of one of Spain's leading female chefs, Carme Ruscalleda. Deeply in tune with the natural cycle of food, Ruscalleda's dishes are highly creative and technical. Her degustation menu includes eight superbly crafted

courses, such as stuffed calamari and Iberian pork shoulder, accompanied by 'micro menus' at either end of the meal, with bite-size surprises like anchovy ice-cream and a tiny brochette of rabbit and kiwi fruit.

76 VUE DE MONDE
Melbourne, Australia
Web: www.vuedemonde.com.au

Testament to the belief that restaurant food can be truly indulgent and unforgettable, Vue de Monde owner-chef, Shannon Bennett, offers quirky Francophile cuisine in an atmosphere of understated luxury. His inspiration comes from recipes dating back hundreds of years to which he adds his own modern twist. Classic ingredients such as Strasbourg foie gras, black Périgord truffles and caviar are presented alongside local produce, and the menu gourmand allows a tailored dining experience specific to each party. Bennett puts Australia firmly on the map for fine dining.

77 IGGY'S
Singapore
Web: www.iggys.com.sg

This tiny restaurant is fast becoming one of Singapore's most famous. Opened by award-winning sommelier and restaurateur Ignatius Chan in 2004, it feels more like a private club than a restaurant. An L-shaped counter that seats 13 takes up the main dining room; these highly coveted seats allow diners the chance to see the action in the kitchen. The menu changes with the seasons, but recent meals have included char-grilled sea bass with truffle gnocchi and rosemary oil; a piña colada soufflé, and champagne jelly and sorbet topped with elderberry foam and lemon zest.

78 ETRUSCO
Athens, Greece
Web: www.ettorebotrini.com

The first branch of Etrusco was set up on Corfu, where it established itself at the forefront of Greek cookery thanks to its impressive line of Italian-influenced dishes. From here it expanded to the Athenian Callirhoe Hotel, finding a foothold in the Greek capital. Since then, chef-owner Hector Botrini and his wife Monica have delighted diners with crayfish and caviar with vodka and fresh lime juice, and squid ink soup with potato purée. They've even devised caviar chocolate for dessert.

79 DE KARMELIET
Bruges, Belgium
Web: www.dekarmeliet.be

De Karmeliet's Belgian gastronomy certainly merits its three-Michelin-star status. It's an accolade that is even more impressive when you consider that head chef Geert Van Hecke was the first Flemish chef to be awarded three stars when he received them in 1996. With a menu he describes as 'international cuisine using local products', De Karmeliet aims to combine French quality with Flemish quality. This has resulted in delicious, but deceptively plain-sounding dishes, such as potato bouillon with shelled shrimps, or cod and toasted sea bass with crust of pistachio and hazelnut.

80 CAFÉ PUSHKIN
Moscow, Russia
Web: www.cafe-pushkin.ru

A trip to Café Pushkin is like stepping back in time: the pre-Revolutionary décor, with French windows, high ceilings and shelves of ancient books are like something out of a Russian novel. Staff members dress like 19th-century servants and the food is fit for a tsar. All the favourites can be found here – blini, caviar and pelmeni, and there's a fine wine list. Prices rise with each floor (there are three) of the restaurant. Open daily and for 24 hours, Pushkin is popular among the business elite and the wealthy youth who come for breakfast after a night out clubbing.

81 IKARUS RESTAURANT IN HANGAR-7
Salzburg, Austria
Web: www.hangar-7.com/ikarus

Built by Red Bull magnate Dietrich Mateschitz, Hangar-7 was created to house his aeroplane collection. With that kind of backing, it's no wonder the hangar also boasts a world-class restaurant. Executive chef, Roland

Trettl, thrives on pressure to produce such high-quality dishes as risotto of squid and saddle of veal. But the restaurant's true selling point is its playful guest-chef concept, allowing the restaurant to broaden its appeal by harnessing ideas from the finest gourmets. Ikarus has extended invitations to the likes of Osteria Francescana's Massimo Bottura and Gerard Depardieu.

82 MAISON PIC
Valence, France
Web: www.pic-valence.com

Preferring to call herself a cook rather than a chef, Anne-Sophie Pic is the fourth-generation head of this family business, which earned three Michelin stars as long ago as 1934 and repeated the feat in 1973. Pic takes a hands-on role in the kitchen, visible from the bright and airy patio that looks out onto a picturesque patio. Favouring what she terms 'feminine simplicity', she eschews over-elaboration for more direct flavours, such as line-caught sea bass with onion preserve and walnut caramel sauce – plus tangy desserts such as Grand Marnier soufflé.

83 L'ATELIER DE JOËL ROBUCHON
London, UK
Web: www.joel-robuchon.com

Super-chef Joël Robuchon opened his London branch in 2006, the same year as his New York equivalent (see number 85 on the list). Like the other six branches, the London restaurant is a testament to Robuchon's ethos of 'simplicity, quality and informality'. Executive chef Frederique Simonin delights the palate with clean, incisive flavours and refreshingly unfussy presentation. Wherever possible, new dishes are developed using British produce. A set lunch and pre-theatre menu (5.30pm to 6.30pm) are available for a reasonable price.

84 LEDOYEN
Paris, France
Web: www.ledoyen.com

Nestled behind a lush veil of trees between Montaigne Avenue and Place de la Concorde, just off the Champs-

Elysées, Ledoyen provides a charismatic introduction to French cuisine in a restaurant that dates back to 1798. Under executive chef Christian Le Squer, who earned his third Michelin star here in 2002, the quality of ingredients is paramount. Born in Brittany on France's northern coast, he is keen to convey his love of the sea, and offers excellent turbot and lemon sole.

85 L'ATELIER DE JOËL ROBUCHON
New York, US
Web: www.joel-robuchon.com

Another of Joël Robuchon's Ateliers, his New York branch is every bit as successful as his restaurants elsewhere. Little wonder, given Robuchon's unique combination of indulgence and minimalism. Executive chef Yosuke Saga makes sure the cuisine measures up with Robuchon's signature dishes, such as truffled mashed potatoes and free-range quail stuffed with foie gras, taking pride of place. As with his other Ateliers, seats are arranged around a spacious counter for a view of the creative process, breaking down the barriers between the kitchen and dining room.

86 LA MAISON DE BRICOURT
Cancale, France
Web: www.maisons-de-bricourt.com

One of three houses overlooking the stunning bay of Mont St-Michel, La Maison de Bricourt is presided over by world-renowned 'king of spice' Olivier Roellinger. He makes great use of the abundance of seafood that can be found in the bay via two exquisite tasting menus that feature dishes such as sea bream roasted with bay leaf and lemon fennel seeds and green tomato jam; and oysters, squid and tender cabbage, 'route of the South Seas', which is flavoured with curry and hazelnut.

87 L'ATELIER DE JOËL ROBUCHON
Las Vegas, USA
Web: www.mgmgrand.com

Yet another of Joël Robuchon's successful Ateliers, this time in Las Vegas's fabulous MGM Grand casino.

Perfect for a break between roulette tables, here it is the dedicated team of Eric Bouchenoire, Philippe Braun and Eric Lecerf that produces all the great Atelier's signature tapas-style portions. Look out for mouthwatering amuse bouches, such as foie gras parfait with port wine and Parmesan foam. The open kitchen overlooked by a circular bar with 36 seats allows clients to follow the service and watch the succession of dishes being intricately arranged. As you would expect, the service is attentive and the wines are tailored to suit the individual meal.

88 PIERRE GAGNAIRE
Hong Kong
Web: www.mandarinoriental.com

Another addition to Pierre Gagnaire's growing portfolio of international restaurants, his eponymous venue in Hong Kong is every bit the haven of luxury that you might expect under head chef (and Pierre Gagnaire protégé) Philippe Orrico. Dishes retain a distinctly French flavour, but with the experimental twist for which Gagnaire is best known. Expect to see some of his classic starters such as pan-fried snails au avert with aubergine marmalade, or mousseline pear and pan-fried foie gras with liquorice butter and hazelnuts. The menu changes with the seasons, meaning dishes never get tired, and there is always the excitement of something new to try.

89 BIKO
Mexico City, Mexico
Web: www.biko.com.mx

A cut above the norm in Mexico City, Biko is run by young chefs Mikel Alonso and Bruno Oteiza, who after years of training in Arzak (see page 46), returned to Mexico to open this Basque-inspired restaurant, which means 'couple' or 'duo' in Euskara, the language of Basque Spain. Living up to its name, it features two menus: one traditional, the other more modern and creative, although in reality, every dish is so inventive it feels unique. Take the alcachofas con almejas, the Basque classic reinterpreted: a tender artichoke heart wrapped in a lightly spiced batter and nestled in a fresh clam shell with reduced broth.

90 LE PONT DE BRENT
Montreux, *Switzerland*
Web: *www.lepontdebrent.ch*

A three-star Michelin chef since 1998, Gérard Rabaey is as sharp as a chef's knife. In 2006, he scored 19 out of 20 points in the *Gault-Millau* guide for the 19th consecutive year, earning him its prestigious Chef of the Year title. He steers a dozen cooks through the exuberant menu of Le Pont de Brent, and many former colleagues have gone on to open their own restaurants. Dishes include a range of fish, cannelloni with veal sweetbreads, and foie gras terrine with figs. Among the dessert choices on offer are coffee ice-cream and rhubarb crumble.

91 COMBAL.ZERO
Rivoli, *Italy*
Web: *www.combal.org*

A visit to Combal.Zero requires you to leave your preconceptions about traditional dining at the door. Head chef Davide Scabin delights in creating a unique gastronomic show that challenges conventional ideas of presentation and eating. Expect your tableware to consist of some unusual tools alongside the cutlery. You'll need a mallet to crack open the 'fossil' course to discover the savoury mix of fish, black truffle and white beans embalmed inside a clay tomb served on a bed of fragrant wood chips. Scabin possesses an astonishing imagination, presenting traditional Piedmont cuisine in ways that continue to surprise and intrigue.

92 WALDHOTEL
Dreis, *Germany*
Web: *www.hotel-sonnora.de*

According to head chef Helmut Thieltges, Waldhotel does not just create dishes; it invents culinary masterpieces. But with only a dozen tables it is hard to ensure a weekend reservation closer than three months to your intended dining date. Customers are advised to either book a room in the hotel, or take a slightly less coveted lunch slot to give themselves a better chance of obtaining a table. Goose liver ravioli with essence of oxtail broth and pigeon with carrot tart are just two of the upmarket meals on offer.

93 JARDINE
Cape Town, *South Africa*
Web: *www.jardineonbree.co.za*

Found in bustling Bree Street, Cape Town, Jardine is the home of one of South Africa's finest chefs, Scottish-born George Jardine. His talent and skills were honed in some of London's finest kitchens such as Novelli and at South Africa's Cellars Hohenort. He prefers not to typecast or label his style of cooking, but admits that it is founded upon contemporary European techniques and South Africa's finest seasonal produce. The dishes speak for themselves, such as tender seared Chalmar ribeye with baked prune and potato galette, onion and bacon jus and roasted poached pears. His cuisine is complemented by an excellent selection of boutique South African wine estates.

94 PLAVI PODRUM
Volosko, *Croatia*
Web: *www.mrvely.com/restaurants-en.html*

Cradled in a picturesque port town, Plavi Podrum offers some of the most evocative and traditional quality seafood cookery to be found anywhere in Europe. So it's little surprise to find that one of the restaurant's staff has the title of being the longest-serving waiter in Croatia, while owner-manager Daniela Kramaric is the nation's champion sommelier. The seasonal menu allows diners to choose from trusty favourites like oysters, shrimp and fish, while more exotic examples include sea-eggs and sea-urchins. Side dishes include nettles, truffles and wild asparagus, and Kramaric is on hand to serve a different wine for every course.

95 GEORGES BLANC VONNAS
Vonnas, *France*
Web: *www.georgesblanc.com*

Tradition and innovation come together at this welcoming auberge 80km from Lyon. Georges Blanc is the fourth generation of the Blanc family to have managed the restaurant in Vonnas since the family first took it over in 1872 and the original restaurant has also been followed by numerous Georges

Blanc shops and restaurants in this small town. His signature style stays true to French tradition, but also incorporates new flavours, such as his torteau gnocchi with a medley of spices. His menu also includes recipes such as crêpes vonnassiennes and roast Sot L'y Laisse chicken that were passed down by the current Georges Blanc's great grandmother.

96 HUBERTUS
Filzmoos, *Austria*
Web: *www.hotelhubertus.at*

The Relais & Châteaux Hotel Hubertus, to give it its full name, is run by highly-rated chef Johanna Maier and her husband, Dietmar. Trained under three-star chef Dieter Müller, currently at the R&C Hotel Schloss Lerbach, Johanna is quite clear that cooking is her life. She is particular about what she calls 'original taste', which is to say that her apple sorbet must carry an intense flavour of the original fruit. For mains, she offers such mouthwatering dishes as saddle of lamb gratin on a bed of peppers, and saltimbocca of monkfish with fiery couscous.

97 COMME CHEZ SOI
Brussels, *Belgium*
Web: *www.commechezsoi.be*

Since it was first established in 1926, Comme Chez Soi has seen four generations of the same family behind the stove. The current head chefs, Pierre Wynants and his son-in-law Lionel Rigolet, have continued a winning tradition. Wynants, in particular, is ceaselessly inventive in his quest for new culinary creations. Dishes such as potato-mousseline with crab, shrimps, Royal Belgian caviar and white oyster butter with chive, or breast of cuckoo from Mechelen with roasted duck liver and reduced raspberry vinegar typify his passion for experimenting with the finest ingredients.

98 ROBUCHON À GALERA
Hotel Lisboa, *Macau*
Web: *www.hotelisboa.com*

It was something of a surprise when Joël Robuchon arrived in Macau with his Robuchon à Galera restaurant, but it has since established itself as a valuable showcase of Western cuisine in the Far East. With dynamic celebrity chef Joël Robuchon at the helm, and his pupil Francky Sembat directing the menu, the restaurant offers a range of high-quality French gastronomy, with some dishes specially adapted into Oriental variations. Starters include fried pigeon eggs with caviar and salmon, lobster broth with ginger, and crispy papillotes of scampi with basil, while veal knuckle braised in Château-Chalon is one of nine main courses.

99 ZUMA
Hong Kong
Web: *www.zumarestaurant.com*

Another success story for chef, proprietor and co-founder Rainer Becker, Zuma Hong Kong is the second of his restaurants to feature on this list even though it only opened a year ago in June 2007. As with Zuma London (see number 64), the cuisine is authentic Japanese, but not strictly traditional. Signature dishes include baby chicken marinated in barley miso, oven roasted on cedar wood, and spicy beef tenderloin with sesame, red chilli and sweet soy. It's a venue to look out for in the future thanks to the high level of its cookery and its popular style of sharing dishes.

100 RESTAURANT ABAC
Barcelona, *Spain*
Web: *www.restaurantabac.com*

One of the most eye-catching regions of one of Europe's finest cities, Barcelona's Gothic Quarter blends classical and modern styles – just like the Restaurant ABAC it is home to. Head chef Xavier Pellicer has coined his own term, 'cuisine d'auteur', to describe his distinctive approach: a carnival of flavour encompassing fennel ravioli, baby goat roasted with kalamata olives, artichokes and foie gras; roasted sea bass with sweet pimientos, and crispy suckling pig. A sample menu allows dining parties to order a range of dishes for everyone to try, and the staff is immaculately presented in designer uniforms.

LIFETIME ACHIEVEMENT AWARD WINNER 2008

Gualtiero Marchesi, the first Italian chef to win three Michelin stars, is this year's recipient of the Laurent-Perrier Lifetime Achievement Award. At 78 years young, Marchesi is by far Italy's most renowned chef, having created a string of award-winning restaurants and the culinary philosophy 'Total Cuisine', as set out in his seminal book, *The Marchesi Code*.

Total Cuisine requires attention to every detail, and when Marchesi opened his first restaurant in Milan in 1977, it was something of a revolution. Within six months, Ristorante Gualtiero Marchesi had earned him his first Michelin star, and by 1985, the restaurant had three – a first for Italy.

In 2004 he helped launch ALMA, the International School of Italian Cuisine. He was also a founder member of Euro-Toques International, the association of European chefs in 1986, the year he became a 'Cavaliere della Republica' (Knight of the Italian republic). In 1993, he moved to the hills of Erbusco, where he spends most of his time today.

Marchesi's cooking is influenced by his love of art, most obviously in dishes inspired by paintings and sculptures and his desire to reinterpret the traditional and familiar in a new light. 'It is important to respect tradition,' he says. 'Only then can you move forward.' In his recipes, he explains, 'I have attempted to bear in mind Goethe's assertion that artists "are not those that say something new but those who know how to say a well-known thing as if it had never been said before".'

His tireless energy shows no sign of waning: he is currently at work on a new restaurant called Marchesino, to open in Milan within the year.

Ristorante Gualtiero Marchesi, Via Vittorio Emanuele 23, 25030 Erbusco, Brescia, Italy +39 03 077 60562

www.marchesi.it

Previous Lifetime Achievement Award winners

2007 Alice Waters Described variously as a visionary, a pioneer, 'the mother of American cooking' and 'the most important figure in the culinary history of North America', Alice Waters (above) is certainly one of the most influential figures in American cooking of the last 50 years.

2006 Albert and Michel Roux Having put their fraternal bond to the ultimate test for four decades and come through with flying colours, the Roux brothers, Albert and Michel, can truly claim to be lifetime achievers.

2005 Paul Bocuse When it came to deciding who would receive the inaugural Lifetime Achievement Award, there was only ever one name on the list. Paul Bocuse, more than any other living chef, has come to be seen as an ambassador for French cuisine.

Thomas Barwick/Getty

PHOTOGRAPHER CREDITS

01_ El Bulli
© Rodrigo Diaz
Wichmann/
DiazWichmann
Photography
02_ The Fat Duck
© Pal Hansen
© Laurie Fletcher/
Restaurant magazine
03_ Pierre Gagnaire
© Laurie Fletcher /
Restaurant magazine
04_ Mugaritz
© Jose Luis López
de Zubiria
© Ander Armendariz and
Guillermo Monford of
Enter Designs SL
05_ The French Laundry and
06_ Per Se
© Deborah Jones
07_ Bras
© Bras
08_ Arzak
© Arzak
09_ Tetsuya's
© Tetsuya's
10_ Noma
© Ditte Isager
© Anders Birch
© Tuala Hjarno/
Photography CPH
11_ L'Astrance
© Francoise Cadot
12_ Gambero Rosso
© Suzanne Mitchell
13_ Gordon Ramsay
Clare Smyth: © Suki
Dhanda/Guardian News
& Media Ltd 2007
© Laurie Fletcher
© Suzanne Mitchell

14_ L'Atelier de Joël Robuchon
© Mr Robuchon Private
Collection
© Laurie Fletcher
© Gerard Bedeau
15_ Louis XV - Alain Ducasse
© T Duval
© Bernard Touillon
16_ St John
Fergus © Guy Drayton
Trevor & Fergus:
© Jason Lowe
Roast Bone Marrow:
© Patricia Niven
17_ Jean Georges
© Jean Georges
18_ Plaza Athénée
© Benoit Peverelli
© Thomas Duval
© Françoise Nicol
19_ Hakkasan
Interiors
©Herbert
Ypma
Head shots
© Frantzesco Kangaris
20_ Le Bernardin
© Nigel Parry
© Shimon & Tammar
© Brigitte Lacombe
21_ Alinea
© Lara Kastner
22_ Le Gavroche
© Laurie Fletcher/
Restaurant magazine
© Richard Gleed
23_ Dal Pescatore
© Dal Pescatore
24_ Le Cinq
© Eric Beaumard
© David Arralz

25_ La Maison Troisgros
© Jérôme Aubanel
26_ El Celler de Can Roca
© El Celler de
Can Roca
27_ Hôtel de Ville – Philippe Rochat
© Marcel Gilliéron
28_ Hof van Cleve
© Jean-Pierre Gabriel
29_ Martìn Berasategui
© José Luis López
de Zubiria
30_ Nobu
© Laurie Fletcher
© Suzanne Mitchell
© Luca Zampedri
31_ Can Fabes
© Can Fabes
32_ Enoteca Pinchiori
© Enoteca Pinchiori
33_ Le Meurice
© Le Meurice
34_ Vendôme
© Althoff Hotel
Collection Headquarters
in Cologne
35_ Schwarzwaldstube Traube-Tonbach
© Hotel Traube-Tonbach
36_ Le Calandre
© www.wowe.it
37_ Chez Panisse
© Platon
© Thomas Heinser
38_ Charlie Trotter's
© Kipling Swehla
© Charlie Trotter's
Restaurant
39_ Chez Dominique
© Sami Repo

40_ D.O.M.
© Alex Atala
41_ Daniel
© Owen Franken
© P Medilek
© M Noguchi
© T Schauer
© Battman
42_ Oud Sluis
© Tony Le Duc
43_ Ristorante Cracco
© Ristorante Cracco
44_ Etxebarri
© Asador Etxebarri
45_ Les Ambassadeurs
© Stéphane de Bourgies
© Grant Symon
46_ L'Arpège
© Stéphane de Bourgies
© Pascal Michaut
47_ Tantris
© Tantris
48_ Oaxen Skärgårdskrog
© Oaxen Skärgårdskrog
49_ Rockpool (Fish)
© Earl Certer
50_ Le Quartier Français
© Le Quartier Français
The Roux brothers, p209:
© Shaun Bloodworth
Gualtiero Marchesi, p208:
© Mads Mogensen
Paul Bocuse, p209:
© Laurie Fletcher

INDEX BY COUNTRY

■ SWITZERLAND

L'Hôtel de Ville –
Philippe Rochat
Le Pont de Brent

■ UK

L'Atelier de Joël
Robuchon
The Fat Duck
Le Gavroche
Hakkasan
Maze
Nobu
Restaurant Gordon
Ramsay
The River Café
The Square
St John
The Waterside Inn
Zuma

USA

Alinea
L'Atelier de Joël
Robuchon
Le Bernardin
Charlie Trotter's
Chez Panisse
Daniel
The French Laundry
Jean Georges
Masa
Nobu
Per Se
WD-50

■ RUSSIA

Café Pushkin

▥ SINGAPORE

Iggy's

■ SOUTH AFRICA

Jardine
Le Quartier Français

■ SPAIN

Akelarre
Arzak

Asador Etxebarri
El Racó de Can Fabes
El Bulli
El Celler de Can Roca
Martín Berasategui
Mugaritz
El Poblet
Restaurant ABAC
Sant Pau

▥ SWEDEN

Esperanto
Oaxen Skärgårdskrog

INDEX BY RESTAURANT

INDEX BY CHEF